THE MISSIONARY, THE VIOLINIST AND THE AUNT WHOSE HEAD WAS SQUEEZED

THE MISSIONARY, THE VIOLINIST AND THE AUNT WHOSE HEAD WAS SQUEEZED

non-fiction by

Keith Harrison

OOLICHAN BOOKS

FERNIE, BRITISH COLUMBIA, CANADA

2010

Library and Archives Canada Cataloguing in Publication

Harrison, Keith
    The missionary, the violinist and the aunt whose head was squeezed / Keith Harrison.

ISBN 978-0-88982-265-8

1. Harrison, Keith--Family. 2. Harrison family. I. Title.

PS8565.A656Z465 2010   C813'.54   C2010-901911-3

We gratefully acknowledge the financial support of the Canada Council for the Arts, the British Columbia Arts Council through the BC Ministry of Tourism, Culture, and the Arts, and the Government of Canada through the Book Publishing Industry Development Program, for our publishing activities.

Cover design: Henning Nielsen

Published by
Oolichan Books
P.O. Box 2278, Fernie
British Columbia, Canada
V0B 1M0

Printed in Canada

This double-looped book of
travel and family history
is a two-fold love letter

For my father, John Robert Harrison
(1915-1984)
and
To my wife, JoAnn

Preface

Although my half dozen books so far have been fiction, mostly novels, I have long been interested in how actual lives get told or shown. Mini-biography is a key element in a dozen *ciné-fiches* I wrote for the National Film Board presentations of such literary figures as Margaret Atwood, Al Purdy, and P. K. Page. An extended essay of mine on the documentary, *Ladies and Gentlemen...Mr. Leonard Cohen*, references how biography gets focused through the lens of autobiography. Another long essay, "Telling the Untellable: Spiegelman's *Maus*," on the comic book artist's rendering of his father's experience of Auschwitz, concerns the fusion within the panels that he draws of portrait with self-portrait. Probably the most important imaginative context for *The missionary, The Violinist, and The Aunt Whose Head Was Squeezed* is my non-non-fiction novel, *Furry Creek*, which uses legal transcripts, letters, manuscripts, interviews, and unpublished poems to explore the life and art and death of Pat Lowther. In a sense, this new project can be considered as a companion piece to that documentary novel. By combining travel with family history, I ended up facing parts of my own familial past that I didn't necessarily want to know about. In reckoning with a world that was simultaneously measuring me, I found out—in a kind of reverse epiphany—that I became less certain of who I am.

LOVE AND WAR IN MELBOURNE

. . . people perched on top of statues and in branches

Saturday, March 15, 2003

The train to Melbourne speeds by yellows, browns, and blacks, evidence of drought and fire that a few months ago threatened Australia's capital, but recent rain has greened patches of the earth. Gum trees appear everywhere—like tired male ballet dancers in torn leotards who keep lifting even as they bend. Reminiscent of the dancey, tendoned arbutus trees back home on Hornby Island, British Columbia, these tensile eucalypts animate this continent of a country. More inhabitants than growths, they look poised to drift away, go walkabout.

I glance down at today's newspaper, *The Age*, and read headlines of places we're headed: an outbreak of dengue fever in Cairns, Queensland, North Korea plans to test-fire more missiles over Japan, fatal car crashes near Venice due to fog. In the Gulf, a war about to explode. Not such a great time to be circumnavigating the globe.

Find myself humming, "Don't Know Why," the title of a gluey ballad sung by Norah Jones that follows my wife, Jo, and me from country to country. Yet there's a design to these disappearing arcs of sky, a double purpose to this being away for five months. It is the wish to experience more of this planet while I still can, and to trace the several, mostly separate journeys

11

my father and his mother and father made across the world's then wide oceans. The restless geometry of their disconnected travels nearly curved them back home. Now, within the itinerary of a round-the-world ticket— valid only if Air Canada avoids bankruptcy?—I can read, in reverse, the incomplete and inadvertent circle shape of their voyaging: Vancouver-Australia-Tokyo-Prague-St. Ives, Cambridgeshire.

The train clatters on towards Melbourne, the city I've always known of from my dead father, and never seen. Before we get there, I try to catch yesterday in my spiral diary. At Canberra, Jo and I had rented gleaming bikes, and rode around the large artificial lake named after the capital's American architect. On this vast site, with its few buildings, I had a sense of vacancy. The two of us crossed the long bridge over Lake Burley Griffin, and pedalled uphill to the grass-covered parliament. "Visiting this gorgeous building is a must," according to *Lonely Planet*. The dug-in, grassed-over setting had definite ecological appeal, but it looked like an elongated white bunker. And contradicting its modest groundedness were four shiny, immense metal legs that supported a gigantic flagpole whose sky-ey claims seemed jokey and dubious. "Its flag alone is about the size of a double-decker bus!" gushed the Australian guidebook, referencing a not-to-be-forgotten Imperial London.

On the steps of the Parliament House, an armed guard in uniform had eyed me uneasily. There's no way to see out except from inside your own head, and on the day after their Prime Minister had, in effect, declared war on Iraq, how was he to know a lone, dark-haired Canadian cyclist wasn't a terrorist? Jo caught up to me on her bike, and the tiny facial muscles of the man relaxed. He nodded towards us, but kept a wary, erect posture. The two of us plunged through a metal detector, abandoned our plastic water bottles, and stepped into a large, bright room forested with stylized gum trees. The understated beauty of these faceted columns, grey-green at the base and creamy white above, re-shapes a classical inheritance for a new habitat. (And it's a possible way for me to think about this journey where, via the past, I'm moving into some kind of future.) Walking on towards the House of Representatives, Jo and I paused at a glassed-in case displaying one of the few surviving copies of the Magna Carta, then stepped down to the visitors' gallery to gaze at a roomful of desks equipped with pull-out keyboards: row upon row of empty seats. Another pleasing chamber in its casual elegance and in its generous yet compact design, but where at this time of international crisis were the voices? Many Australians believed no real debate had taken place about their part in the invasion of Iraq because it was a decision kept internal to John Howard's Cabinet. Returning re-doubled is my earlier sensation of the void. Canberra (like Ottawa) is a compromise location whose political significance derives from its previous unimportance. It occupies a vast inland space that's not too close to either of the rival coastline cities, Sydney and Melbourne.

When Jo and I exited the parliament building, we saw young protesters in the middle distance, standing in vigil in front of a colourful anti-war banner that stretched nearly horizon-wide. (A week ago, riding in from the Sydney airport, I had noticed a graffito painted on a factory wall: "Bush is poison.") Now, with our backs turned to Australia's Parliament House, we looked out at Canberra's sculpted and panoramic newness—accentuated by the scattered saplings and the huge gaps between buildings—and, what earlier felt like emptiness, now registered as openness: unconstrained vistas in every direction.

Jo and I continued on our bike tour of the capital, backtracking to the National Archives. At the reception counter, a woman in a summery blazer came over and helped me search for the name of my Australian grandmother, Ethel Mercer, who I must have met once or twice as a kid, but who I can't remember. There was a possible listing as next of kin for a serviceman, but since he was from Queensland, not the State of Victoria, this Ethel Mercer wasn't the one. We biked on to the National Library where a slim, black-haired woman, Jackie, tried to find Ethel in secondary sources, but, again, no luck. Partly to reassure myself, I produced a folded, rain-softened xerox of an article titled "Melbourne's Master Musicians" (dated December 23, 1939) that I'd been carrying near the top of my backpack: "once Australia's outstanding woman violinist, now living in Canada." But no one could locate her name. Had I been a victim of vanity, buying into a flattering family myth of talent and fame?

Feeling restless and tired of trying to reconstruct yesterday, I set my notebook aside and walk forward through the swaying train. On a small, flickering screen in the dining car is *Rabbit-Proof Fence*. This Australian film about the seizure of aboriginal kids is a variant on Canada's sad history of residential schools. Standing, watching, balancing, I forget immediately that the three young girls trying to elude their captors and cross impossible distances to get back home are pretending— are actors. The movie picks up a hint of the glaucous sky passing by outside the moving windows.

At a conference in Hawai'i, where this trip started, I learned that the native word there for whites is "Howlies": "those who steal our breath away." And I wonder again at the harsh paradox of how in my own country so much anguish and lostness came from a distorted idea of caring. My eyes flick back to the haunting images on the small screen, and I struggle to listen to the low, tinny audio over the cheery voices of diners and the clicking, shifting sounds of the train. My father, I remember, told me with a certain pride that his nickname at school was Abo, short for aboriginal, because he tanned so darkly. I recall some of the false ethnicities I've been labeled with: Luigi in high school, an anti-Semitic comment directed my way in a pool hall, and once a white-haired woman praised me by saying my English was very good for a Mexican. I need to watch this film of unbelonging from the beginning.

Walking backward through the long undulating line of linked cars, I think of how yesterday in Canberra, riding along the lakefront, Jo and I paused at the National Museum of Australia, which had just closed. Its outside had definite pizzazz with a swoopy roof, bold reds, bright blacks, sandy gold, an upright block of startling white, idiosyncratic windows, some gleaming metal with sharp bends, an updated barber pole next to a palm tree, and in the forecourt beautiful motifs evocative of Aboriginal song-lines. Jo really liked the building's fizzy energy, and I did too, even if it felt a bit noisy—like the festive pressure on New Year's Eve to talk too loud, drink too much, and kiss everybody. According to a too-talkative bus driver, it's not only the design of the museum in Canberra that's controversial and unloved by some: "Some people felt it pandered too much to our aborigines." Silence had fallen over his handful of passengers. (What word did I wince at more: "pandered" or "our"?)

My eyes, chugging on their way to Melbourne, long to touch all those locked up aboriginal works: bark painting, printed fabrics, painted canvasses, burial poles. But likely never will—I'm missing Australia even in the act of looking.

Retreating to my seat, I wordlessly greet Jo and pick up Peter Carey's *True History of the Kelly Gang*, and consider again its epigraph taken from William Faulkner, "The past is not dead. It is not even past." A wide swath of railway tracks appears. I'm pretty good at fighting off the seductions of synecdoche, at not mistaking the part for the whole, but wish the first Aborigine I saw was not a red-eyed drunk, alone in a Sydney park, standing near some trees, staring at nothing. As the train nears Melbourne, I read the last pages of the novel. Maybe as someone whose cultural icons are red-coated Mounties, not murderous outlaws—and one conscious of the coming war motivated by the thirst for oil and the wounds of New York—I just can't connect the hypersensitive younger

Ned Kelly to the killing machine he becomes. The train slows, and we're in the city where, in 1880, the notorious bushranger, Ned Kelly, was hanged. Was Ethel already born here?

Jo and I help each other lift on our backpacks, then walk outside the train station into the city that might have been my birthplace. A surge of boisterous people hurry across the wide street, converge on the Telstra Dome where a season of "footie" is about to start. On TV the game has an intriguing strangeness: the fat, startlingly white football, the physical mayhem of burly players on the oval pitch in tumbling, desperate pursuit of the ball, supervised only by the sharp, controlling hand gestures of the small, capped referee clad in impeccable white, and above the fray, the perfect high white posts. Footie, the legacy of a convict colony transformed into sport? These very upbeat fans of Australian Rules Football in their pent-up eagerness don't trample us, or even brush our bodies. Seemingly without the dark passion Canadians bring to hockey, these faces are sun-tanned and sunny. With ice hockey, there's a residue of seriousness, of wintry survival. I unfold the Melbourne map, and Jo immediately figures out how to get us to the Hotel Y on Elizabeth Street—she then helps out two English tourists needing directions.

On the Melbourne city bus, I experience a twinge of disloyalty to my ancestral past, to the vanished lives of my father's parents that I hope to reanimate. The buildings here in the historic grid are—a favorite adjective of guidebooks—"handsome," while Sydney excited us with its ragged, pulsing coastline. Flying in from New Zealand at sunset, looking down on Sydney's endless harbour, with surfing beach after fabulous surfing beach, we were impatient to land. The city itself had in George Street a strong melodic line to follow—a variegated length to wander away from without getting lost. We could catch the loopings and criss-crosses of boats in harbour riffs, our eyes tearing happily under the windy ozone sky, before coming back to Sydney's main groove and artery with salt sea on our breaths. With its urban edge always shifting, moving to a lunar rhythm, Sydney was jazzy. From the bus window, Melbourne by contrast appears to have the orderliness of surveyed ground, of agriculture. The clarity of well-proportioned stone buildings, the symmetry of measured intersections. The sedate, uninterrupted perspectives offered by these broad streets make this city more akin to classical music. Although Ethel (allegedly) performed here as a concert violinist—and I'm transfixed when Glen Gould plays Bach—I'm more attuned to the atonal surprises of Thelonius Monk. Maybe Sydney with its kinetic coastal setting just grabs me more because I grew up near the beaches of Vancouver. Is travel merely a strange way to encounter the familiar?

From our high window in the rear of the Hotel Y, Jo and I look at shed roofs and a vast area of wet pavement that Jo identifies as Queen Victoria Market. She wants to go there tomorrow morning and look for "blundies"—the now fashionable workboots that in Peter Carey's novel are coveted by a young Ned Kelly, whose mentor in exasperation finally tells him: "I'll buy you adjectival effing elastic sided boots."

Jo and I decide to go out into the cooling air of evening, and wander into a district with Greek street signs. In *Melbourne Street Life*, Andrew Brown-May says Greeks dominated the hawking of fish and fruit in the early part of the twentieth century, and were racially vilified. Along with other southern Mediterranean people, they were later solicited as immigrants under the White Australia Policy, and now constitute the third largest gathering of Greeks in the world after Athens and Thessaloniki. It's good to know categories of national belonging are, like Blundstone boots, elastic-sided—can be stretched to accommodate a broader notion of humanity. We pass record stores cranking Greek music out the open doorways, and decide to eat supper at the Stalagtite. From our tiny spot in the corner, having ordered lamb souvlakis along with a carafe of red wine, we watch as a dozen people at a long banquet table shout exuberantly in English and Greek. Families with children occupy the other tables, and I'm suddenly conscious of our two grown sons on the far side of the International Dateline. Yet I also become half-immersed in this room's atmosphere of celebration, created by lively, bilingual people taking pleasure in good food and drink and themselves.

It's spattering rain outside, but I'm quietly delighted now to be among these voices and this laughter, in the city of my own dim origins. Melbourne has to be a place of romance. It's here that my father's mother and father fell in love.

Sunday, March 16

Tess Brady, the writer, comes by the hotel, and we head south on the tour she's volunteered to give to a couple of strangers. She has a great laugh and wears a very cool top with small, yellow-green squares against a woodsy-green background. We all chatter easily while Tess keeps missing turns. She points out Federation Square—a series of zinc, sandstone, and glass buildings covered in crazy tiles and triangles—a bold exhibition space with boyish energy. I think of the impassive neo-Gothic Parliament Buildings in Ottawa, and wonder if Canadians are more sombre than Australians—or if all such big statements about national character have to be hallucinatory.

We leave Melbourne's central grid, cross over the Yarra River on Princes Bridge, and halt at the Southgate arts complex. Tess mentions that live drama is one of the reasons she likes Melbourne, a city she moved to three years ago. We stare for awhile at the Malthouse, the new home of Playbox Theatre Company and Chunky Moves Dance Company. Looking through Canadian lenses, I sense Australian architects maybe feel the weight of originality too much, given their proximity to one of the few iconic buildings of the twentieth century, Utzon's hooded Opera House in Sydney. Designed by a Dane who—

fired before its opening—never returned to this continent.

I shake off thoughts of Sydney as Tess drives us further south and east of Melbourne to Halfmoon Bay. This scoop of bright ocean, part of the immense Port Phillip Bay, is the geographical reason for my grandparent's city. Glinting cars fill the small lot down by the pier, so we park illegally by some boat trailers. On the shoreline stand colourful, newly painted "bathing boxes": wooden shacks with no water or electricity that now go for 80 or 90 thousand dollars, according to Tess who's just co-authored a book called *The Girl's Guide . . . to Real Estate.* We then head north, to the beach suburb of St. Kilda. Once the place for genteel Victorians to take the sea air, it became run-down in the 60's and 70's, but is, again, an "in" place, partly due to "The Secret Life Of Us", a popular TV show set here. Tess points out an apartment block at 14a Acland Street, whose exterior is used as a location shot, and I wonder why there is no Canuck equivalent to this series that's apparently noted for its realism, about young Aussies who're unsure of their futures. We cross over the road to a restaurant, Cicciolina, where two people are having coffee in the semi-sunlight, but when the three of us sit down at the second sidewalk table, we're told only four outside customers are permitted. We shrug, go inside, and I reflect on how this very law-abiding country began as a penal colony.

Afterwards, on the way back to the car, Tess points to the high, bright façade of Luna Park, where a massive human mouth forms the fun entrance to rides and entertainments. Opened to the public in 1912,

Luna Park was one of Melbourne's best-known meeting places, and Tess says my grandmother would likely have visited it. Now it is the site of an annual singles ball, Desperate and Dateless, that Tess tells us she's been to. Jo and I quiz her about the manuscript she's just sent off, *The Girl's Guide . . . Work and Life to Careers*. With a focus on careers as reflective of personality types, she and her fellow writer have invented twenty-nine categories in all, such as Gatekeeper and Host. This practical and satisfying notion is that a career might match people's jobs to their favorite role.

We stop for a late lunch at Williamstown, historically a significant port on the western side of Port Phillip Bay—almost directly across from St. Kilda. Walking through a beachside park, I pause to look at some strikingly fine bowls made from red gum trees. They remind me of arbutus and home, and how, like Australia, our island has the shape of a wonky boomerang. On Hornby Island, the new day always returns as wood. Dim forms of trees reach out from the charcoal sky, stretch up, and stand. I usually get up and wash my face in the cool water of the sink set into the countertop of glued-up, finger-width strips of alder—generally considered scrap wood but in our island home the diverse grains and alternating hues disclose an unexpected loveliness. Another link to Australia is the in-laid line of black-brown eucalyptus that gives a warning contrast to the once whitish beech flooring which the sun has now turned a warm yellow—and marks the descent into the low-ceilinged dining-room. Seated at the round table of bird's eye maple, I can look out beyond the untreated curved cedar deck to a very large, very graceful arbutus that was born before Columbus. Like Michelangelo's David, it is so aesthetically pleasing that its huge larger-than-life scale continually surprises the eye. On the edge of a cliff, rooted in conglomerate rock, it leans south out over Tribune Bay, a connecting body of water that (like myself) is exposed to distant influences both south and east (my father, a student in Melbourne, born in Tokyo). Hornby Island, itself, began in the southern hemisphere—one of the ancient volcanic islands of Wrangellia that with geologic slowness rode north across the equator on the Pacific Ocean plate.

Half a dozen mature, second-growth conifers are visible in the foreground, and their lower trunks rise branchless, echoing the round barkless posts that hold up the squared-off beams of our wooden and glass structure which owes as much to the homes of Haidas as to the spareness of Japanese architecture. The Douglas firs, reminders of the external, living origins of my house, also point to my dead father's work with books and newsprint as a teacher and a journalist, and to his later job for a forestry company that for marketing purposes re-branded hemlock as Alaska White Pine. But it is to the magnificent, uncommercial arbutus tree my gaze again and again returns. Of no interest to loggers, this hard tendony wood keeps on turning and flexing even after it is felled. Arbutus has only the drama and uselessness of beauty.

I pick up a bowl whose rounded, thick-lipped glow pulls me close. The man who turned this red gum into art watches me rotate the smooth form to catch the light falling on us. Reluctantly, because we're backpacking for several more months, I return the bowl to its bearded maker. Then Tess, Jo, and I check out several lunch possibilities before deciding to eat at Al Porto Vecchio. Did Ethel Mercer ever walk through its old, stone-arched doorway? We choose an outside table shaded by a tree, and select a bottle from the long list of wine. The young blonde waitress returns to say it's unavailable, so we choose another bottle, an Australian red. She recommends that we order a "back-up." It seems a ludicrous concept, but what do I know? She quickly returns with our third "choice," which tastes like kit wine. Somehow, we've found ourselves in an episode from *Fawlty Towers*—or is it the Monty Python cheese skit? As we watch the shifting light on the flat sea, and sip the monotone wine, Tess talks a little about the reasons for *TEXT*, Australia's electronic creative writing journal, which she co-edits. With regard to my non-fiction novel, *Furry Creek,* Tess says that I could tell a story if I wanted to. Have to like her subtle directness.

No surfers on the smooth waters of Port Phillip Bay, but just out there somewhere, in the mid-nineteenth century, prison hulks were moored. In *The Fatal Shore* Robert Hughes tells how the convicts floating off Williamstown were weighed down with irons, fed rotten victuals, and whipped, a warship anchored nearby to drown all the prisoners if they mutinied. A bitter irony, given that Britain founded this distant colony to do away with hulks crammed with convicts.

Our victuals finally show up, but no napkins or cutlery. We request some but the apologetic waitress tells us there's a large party upstairs, and we'll have to wait for knives and forks. I can see Tess's cheeks pale with anger, but the afternoon's too full of sunshine to get significantly upset, and in a few minutes a pile of cutlery is thrown down on the table—enough for six people. To my surprise, the margherita pizza is delicious. Still learning to read this page of the world.

Tess drives us back to Melbourne, where—in her favorite role as Hostess?—she insists on showing us one more sight, the bohemian inner suburb of Fitzroy. It's a little north-east of the city grid, with trendy shops and small galleries, and at a corner bar we drink a very fine bottle of red wine from Oz. How can a stranger in one day metamorphose into a companion? Will Jo and I ever see her again?

Back at the Hotel Y, the two of us watch a report on a war conference with Bush and Blair and the Spanish leader that will take place in the Azores. Despite all the American arm-twisting, only four countries have agreed to invade Iraq. We're relieved that Canada, in the absence of a UN resolution, has not yet joined "the coalition of the willing." The fraught news of the approaching Gulf War creates a weird disconnect between the fun day Tess bestowed on us and the unhappy world history about to happen.

Monday, March 17

Bush has given Saddam a 24-hour ultimatum to disarm. With the UN inspectors leaving Iraq immediately (due to the coming war), how can any possible disarmament be verified? Another morning story refers to an acute respiratory virus from Asia that has left two dead in Canada. It sounds a lot like what did in Jo's father: bronchial organizing obliterans pattern. It's supposed to be 33 degrees and sunny in Melbourne. Already, the day feels surreal.

We catch the cream and green #8 tram going south on Swanston Street. We're on a scouting expedition to Melbourne Grammar School, where my father, John, and his younger brother, Noel, were students. The two little boys in my photo hold hands in front of a sylvan screen, and smile with lips closed. They wear dark shorts and knee-socks and, against the collared white shirts, ties that look cut off—missing the triangular point. The polished leather, ankle-high boots have rounded toes, and an extraordinary number of eyelets laced tight. My dad's face, under glossy black hair, could be that of John-Paul, our first son.

Jo and I get off the tram at Domain Road, then walk east through the hot bright air, the treed and grassy expanse of the Royal Botanic Gardens to our left. Dad spoke about the intense heat on a sheep farm where he worked as a drover one Australian summer, on vacation from Melbourne Grammar School. The first building we approach has a plaque with the name of the local member of parliament—John Howard! I glance around, expecting security guards, but see only school kids in uniforms moving leisurely across the expansive playing fields. Never having gone to a private school, I strain to understand what this one was like. How has Melbourne Grammar School produced half of Australia's Prime Ministers? Dark-brown brick buildings with Victorian spires, domes, and towers.

Uncle Noel's recollection helps me partway inside:

> *The senior boys in the long dorm would require that the underlings would run the gauntlet, up and back between their beds, while they with their kangaroo tails, wet towels rolled into tail-like form, would chastise us, en passant.*

What training in intimacy could a male boarding school offer? If my father suffered the sexual harm often reported in such settings, he never mentioned it. (Though he once instructed my brother and me when we were kids to kick any pervert in the balls.)

Jo and I continue walking around the school's perimeter. At Domain Street (as distinct from Domain Road), I try to guess where, for a year or so, my father and his brother and their mother lived together. Noel recalls a single-storey house at the end of the school grounds that now may be a heritage building. Jo takes pictures of several possibilities: that one, with yellow trim and white-painted brick, or the place called

"Ravenswood," or this one, with star-like iron fretwork curving down from the verandah. We stroll on through the Royal Botanic Gardens, and at the Astronomy Centre eat a sandwich outdoors, then continue our walk past hundreds of fruit bats hanging upside down from ·denuded trees. The path takes us by Ornamental Lake and the Temple of the Winds whose names are more picturesque than their settings, then west along the Yarra River, and at a small bridge we split up for the afternoon. We've been travelling together so long, I feel a flicker of anxiety at even such a brief separation. Decades together doesn't mean forever. When my parents divorced, all that I knew to be true became a lie. Love can one day go out for a walk and never come back.

At our Hornby Island domain, a couple of couples look out over the sea. From our bedroom window we can watch a dark, rough-barked vertical fir being squeezed in an ecstatic arbutus embrace—whose two smooth red limbs are flung exuberantly upwards. Even nearer to the water, a second, smaller pair of trees shares a habitat. Edging over the 200-foot escarpment, a smaller arbutus wraps its arms round a lean fir whose roots—due to erosion of the stony cliff-face—dangle mostly in the moist air above the Pacific Ocean.

I cross over to the north side of the Yarra to check out the Rod Laver Tennis Centre, where the Australian Open is played. Today, however, they're setting up for a performance by Riverdance, yet old tennis photos line the curving walls, giving off an elegiacal half-life. The dancers with their stiff upper bodies look immobile next to the swooping artistry of the youthful Rocket Rod Laver. A haunting outdatedness to this legendary man who, just nine inches over five feet, won the Grand Slam twice, and reputedly, had a lefty serving arm that was twice the size of his right. The camera's eye says otherwise. I jot down a few details in my notebook, deforming experience into material. Part of the reason Jo's not keen to be written about?

I catch a tram north, get off near the Victoria State Library, and climb the wide marble stairs. Walking past the special exhibit on Ned Kelly, I turn left, go through a short hall, and enter the Australian research room. On microfiche, almost right away, I see the name of my grandmother, twice. And a librarian shows me a reference to a composition for violin and piano dedicated to "Miss Ethel Mercer." Hurriedly, I scan the catalogue, but still can't come up with a birth certificate. But her marriage is listed, in 1914. A refusal to accept that The Great War was about to extinguish millions of lives? Isn't it always Love against Death, for our jostling species, Eros against Thanatos?

I pull off the shelf the small cardboard box of *Table Talk* for 1899—two years before Australia became a country—and carry the microfilm roll over to the reader machine. A male librarian helps me load the heavy black tape, then comes back and adjusts the machine, reminding me how to focus. I speed the film towards December 14, 1899. It shudders to a halt. A dark-haired woman holds a violin. She looks exactly like my sister, Joan. In a gulp, I swallow down the type below her photograph:

> "Miss Ethel Mercer, the promising violinist, who has made some very successful appearances,

received her first lessons from Mr. Cook, of Ipswich, England. On her arrival in Melbourne she became a pupil of Mr. Henry Curtis, and to him gives the chief credit of her success. Her first introduction to the public was at the Exhibition concerts in 1893. Since then she has played at the Melbourne Philharmonica concerts, the Victoria Musical Society concerts, the Beechworth Liedertafel, and many other places, all her performances being marked by a depth of feeling and skilful execution."

I press the square print button, listen to whirring sounds, and the machine slides out a picture with thin horizontal white lines. In my hands I have an image of my youthful, childless grandmother.

I check out the second newspaper reference to Ethel Mercer, in *The Weekly Times,* 20 May 1905, searching the pages of this issue on the machine twice, but find nothing. Maybe an insert has dropped out and disappeared. It's nearing closing time, so I hustle up to the second floor. The librarian hands me some sheet music: "BERCEUSE," with a dedication at the top, "To Miss Ethel Mercer." Why a lullaby? Was he that much older than her? Does "berceuse" sidestep the romance implicit in, say, "nocturne"? "For Violin & Piano by H. Curtis." Was Henry Curtis in love with Ethel? The price is 2/-net. The composition begins "*andante tranquillo,*" but later, there are several notations for "*cresc[endo].*" A swelling passion? The format of the sheet music is awkward, but I manage to xerox half of the eight-page work before running out of time and coins. If these two music lovers had gotten together, I wouldn't be alive.

Elated, I stride the few blocks to the hotel. The photo and sheet music mean the family past hasn't been obliterated. I show Jo my treasures, and she describes Ethel Mercer's dress as having leg-o'mutton sleeves, with a full flounce below the elbow, and points out that if it were around the wrist, my grandmother wouldn't be able to play the violin. Jo also thinks there's lace on the bodice and pleats on the sleeves, along with a full silk skirt, but it's hard for us to make out the details in what is a xerox of a microfiche of old newsprint pages in which I keep seeing my sister.

We catch a not-bad episode of *The Secret Life Of Us*, and recognize some of the exterior shots of St. Kilda. Then the news, reporting that Heath Ledger, the star of the just-released movie, *Ned Kelly*, will speak at the anti-war rally scheduled for Thursday. Somehow, this heart-throb who can embody Australia's killer male icon is also able to express the strong pacifist tendencies of this country. Ledger, like this continent, must be large enough to display the contradictions that make us human.

I make some notes on the day, and think of my father's writings on Australia.

THE SUN BLAZES DOWN ON

"AUSTRALIA'S CHRISTMAS DAY"

(by John Harrison)

The Hamilton Spectator, December, 1939

On a Sheep Farm at the Antipodes, Although Turkey,

Plum Pudding and the Rest of the Trimmings Are All

Eaten With Gusto, the Chief Problem Is Keeping Cool

With a Shade Temperature in the Hundreds

Christmas day broke clear and bright with not a cloud in the sky to suggest the coming of the long promised rain. By 7 o'clock the heat on the veranda was intolerable and the two boys went inside to get dressed. Once more the sky was a brilliant blue and the sun poured down mercilessly on the paddocks. The view from the house did not in any way present the usual white and green of an Old Country Christmas. The fields were covered with a grayish dust and what appeared to be a sprinkling of grass

of a deadened yellow colour which despite its scarcity was sufficient to feed the sheep and cattle. A few greenish blue gum trees, a clump of apple trees and a field of lucerne provided the only relief from the brown scorched earth.

At the table the presents were opened and every one looked longingly at Christmas cards which showed snow-bound English homes. After breakfast the boys went out to visit the various paddocks, to turn on the windmills in case a breeze should spring up, and to see that the watering troughs were full. Although it was only nine o'clock, even at an easy trot both horses and riders broke out into a sweat. Along the paths, which led over the fields, the dust was fetlock deep and behind each horse a cloud of dust rose up. . . ."

Tuesday, March 18

Jo and I meander through Queen Victoria Market, eyeing the enticing food. We pick a simple take-out lunch, then walk a little south and west to Flagstaff Gardens where we eat on the grass and watch a game of netball. Unlike basketball, the rules disallow dribbling—a useful encouragement to passing and team play. Inside the outdoor court on this historic hill, across from the old burial grounds, alert teenage girls run with fierce delight. Before the advent of the telegraph, the tall white flagstaff here signalled the arrival of distant ships. Lazing around in the Melbourne heat feels great until I check my watch, and start to get nervous: in two hours, I have to give a presentation at Einstein's Bistro.

At 2:40 Jo and I are at the curb outside the front door of the Hotel Y, waiting for the poet, Judith Rodriquez, who phoned to say she would arrive at 2:45. At about 2:50 Jo goes back inside to see if there's a message. A friend warned me that Judith Rodriguez and Tess Brady were not the best of friends, and I wonder what that is about even as I prepare to play the role of Canadian diplomat. Around 3:00 Jo leaves me standing outside, sweating, while she sits down on a sofa in the lobby. At about 3:10 Judith arrives, shakes our hands, makes a brusque apology, puts her ancient leather gloves back on, and we race off into the humid heat. She's tall, and despite being sixty-seven with some kind of hip replacement or arthritic knee, she's absolutely unstoppable. Judith rushes ahead, then quickly brakes, cuts off honking cars, then accelerates with gusto. But we fail to get out of traffic that's drifting geologically north. On an impulse, Judith decides it will be faster to take a freeway far off to our right— somehow she zooms diagonally through several lanes and squeezes into the exit. Not much later, we get out at Deakin University where we are confronted by a stunning anti-war poster: the nozzle of a gas pump with its shiny trigger presses against the forehead of an Arab boy with big, chocolate eyes.

Judith introduces us to a few of her colleagues, and gives me a copy of Deakin's creative writing publication, *Verandah*, along with an anthology, *On Murder: True Crime Writing in Australia*, which includes her poem, "The hanging of Minnie Thwaites." Then she leads me—not to the scaffold but—to a large room with a many-windowed wall, Einstein's Bistro. Though thirsty, I decline a beer and, after Judith's introduction, begin a mini-lecture, "The Poets Steal Canadian Fiction," sketching out to about sixty people how Leonard Cohen, Joy Kogawa, Margaret Atwood, Anne Michaels, Marilyn Bowering, and Michael Ondaatje have through a lyric inflection made the Canadian novel prominent internationally. But the silence of the audience seems to refute this claim: have they never heard of these writers? A little anxiously, I segue into a reading from my non-fiction novel, *Furry Creek*, about a murdered poet, Pat Lowther:

. . . the round bodies of trees. The woven strips of cedar bark, the grey-green smoothness on alder, the scab-like plates for pine, the creamy-white and peelable sheets covering birch, the scales on spruce, the deep ridges of old Douglas Fir trees, and hemlock with patches like human skin cells.'

The audience **is** either quietly attentive or comatose. Afterwards, I field half a dozen questions, then talk with several individuals who approach. One woman says she really liked the passage about decay ("and I breathe in ozone, and drying kelp thrown up by the ocean, the lovely smell of cedar, the funk of ferns, deep mossy dampness, and all the wet, indiscriminate decay of growing things"). Another listener advises me to swallow some of the letters when pronouncing "Melbourne."

Cars everywhere, as Jo and I set off with Judith for her home. At an intersection, a male driver shouts across to us that we have a flat tire. "That's a big help," Judith declares, and keeps on going. We flap-flop-flap through a red light. I offer my services, but Judith says her daughter who is good at these things can fix the tire when we get to her place, which we do pretty quickly. The house has fine woodwork, stained glass, and books galore. While I already knew Judith's knowledge of literature to be wide-ranging, detailed, and incisive, I did not anticipate this truly vast collection of Canadian writings.

For a late dinner, she recommends an Indian restaurant in Box Hill, and phones for a taxi. We go outside, sit on the collapsing stone wall of her verandah, but nobody shows up. I suggest we call back, so Judith re-enters her house, a figure to be reckoned with, but re-emerges abashed. She reports that the dispatcher berated her, "You shouldn't have waited so long to call again." At last, we arrive at the restaurant, Bollywood, where we wait a bit for a table, then have a fine dinner that's additionally spiced by Judith's piquant comments and sharp queries.

After we say thank you and farewell to Judith near the Mont Albert station, Jo and I descend the stairs to catch the commuter train. In this day of waiting that has turned to dark, I find some artificial light and glance at the beginning of the book Judith has given me. Her dramatic monologue about an actual Melbourne murderess, Minnie Thwaites, complements what I read from today: "I am washed under Princess Bridge with its decency of lamps." I'm pleased to be now "local" enough to pick up on Judith's substitution of "Princess" in place of "Princes" for the bridge across the Yarra. By re-naming Melbourne's historic access and exit, she suggests the gap between a fantasy princess and the despised, terrifyingly human, Minnie Thwaites. During this train ride, I'm half-haunted by the character's damp, omnipresent voice of menace and candour.

It's midnight before we make it back to the Hotel Y, exhausted. Mel-brn. Melb-rn. Melb-n?

38

Wednesday, March 19

A fine grey dust lies on the xeroxes by the open window—ash blown from a nearby fire or some distant volcano?

A woman from Deakin University phones to ask me to evaluate a creative writing thesis, "Madonna of the Eucalypt," about journeying, both geographical and spiritual. Is it a prior mapping out of what I might try to do? And I'd like to find out more about Alfred Deakin, the notable Old Melburnian who helped create the Australian Federation. With a good-bye to Jo, I catch the familiar #8 tram for Melbourne Grammar School.

I get off and enter a single-storey bluestone building. Unopened on a table is today's newspaper, but I'm more interested in the framed vintage photos on the walls. Irrationally, I hope to spot my father's schoolboy face with its serious smile, or perhaps Noel's angled, impish head:

> *The trick was to stay in bed as late as possible prior to breakfast at 8 o'clock. A time-saver was to have one's tie looped around one's shirt collar, simply to be tightened. After the required but perfunctory run through the shower downstairs, a scrambled clothing would get one to the dining hall just as the bell sounded. Those who could refine this art seemed to achieve a special status.*

A slender man, Gordon Sargood, greets me and leads me to his office. For forty years, he taught history and coached rugby at MGS, and now is the school archivist. Gordon is helpful, observant, pleasant, and forthcoming with his good memories of a year spent in North America, and for my visit he has located the school contacts at the time John and Noel were students here. Both addresses are in St Kilda (*The Secret Life Of Us*). I'm a little self-conscious sitting in his office with no tie and running shoes, and remember hitting a teacher's fast-moving car with a snowball and getting the strap. Noel recalls being caned by a teacher who *would invariably have us bend over the waste paper basket, telling us to gaze into the crystal ball to see what the future held in store.* Gordon gives me a xeroxed summary of my father's life:

HARRISON, John Robert, son of Rev Ernest Reed Harrison; b 1915; *adm* Wad 1922; Left 1922; *re-adm* 1927; Sen Schl 1929; School Hse; Rusden & Chas Hebden Schols; L.C. 1931; Pro 1933; Univ of Brit Columbia: B.A.; Blue Rugby; Univ of Toronto, M.A.; Blue Rugby; Mgr Industrial Relations, Alaska Pine & Cellulose Ltd, Vancouver, B.C.;2nd World War: 1940-45; R.C.A.F.; Served Canada; A.C.2-Sqdn/Ldr; Coastal Comnd, 9 Br & 160 Br; M.I.D.; *m* Margaret, d of J.I. Reid.

Gordon explains that "Wad." is an abbreviation for "Wadhurst," the primary school, and that my father was only six or seven the first time he came here.

Since the rest of his family remained in Japan, he must have been lonely. A small boy all by himself for an entire year? At age eleven or twelve, Dad was re-admitted, Gordon informs me, and in Sixth Form he ranked second and won two scholarships. In 1933, the year my father left Melbourne Grammar School, he was a "Pro," which Gordon interprets for me as "Probationary," or second to the Prefect. As in a British public school, the programme John Robert Harrison took was straight classics: Greek, Latin, and English. During the last several years at the school, he and Noel boarded: *Somewhat uniquely, I would think, John and I had no direct contact with our parents from April 1929 till May 1933, when mother came to take us to Canada.*

Gordon has an appointment to keep at eleven, but I'm in no hurry to leave. He has been generous and precise with information, but I want more. How could they not have been sad? No class photographs, it seems. We shake hands and Gordon invites me to look around the school, but I feel like an interloper among the blue-blazered students in ties, and go quickly. *Of course there was caning...* Noel's rebelliousness, a quality we might share as second brothers. But his prevailing memories of Melbourne Grammar School are much more benign than the boarding school recollections that focus on bullying and misery. For Noel, it was an experience—especially the rowing—that he loved intensely: *When John and I were taken out of school in Melbourne to come to Vancouver and continue our education there...I sort of wept my guts out practically.*

Dad's overall experience of school in Melbourne must have been more mixed, given his initial separation as a little kid from his family. I board the tram taking me back to the Hotel Y, and try to recall where I was at his age, and what it felt like. My very first memory is of a lurch of sudden air, on the float plane going up from Vancouver to Alert Bay. I was a four year old kid way back then, telling his mom he was going to be sick. The pilot slid open a panel in the floor—at least that's how I remember this. The water, clear as glass, coming closer and closer. Mom held my arm very tight as I leaned out over the rectangular hole of ocean, too scared to puke. I was terrified I was going to fall right into that deep shine. The plane hit the hard wetness and zipped through the spray, with Cormorant Island just ahead. At the dock, we got out and I stood on a fat, rocking pontoon. "Do you want to be sick?" Not really. But a thin trickle from inside was thrown out into the air where it floated on the surface of the clean water.

On northern Vancouver Island, near the logging camp at Port McNeill, I was a kid riding in the back seat on a road that kept curving. Out of nowhere—except boulders and trees—I announced, "There's a boogeyman around the next corner." As we came around the bend, there, in a clearing, a black bear, hunkered down on all fours. Not huge huge, but *big*, with real fangs and claws, and it turned its head to look at us as our car slowed. My dad and mom laughed, and we drove on. My brother and kid sister **kept** silent, stunned even more than me. I was stuck to the seat, but bathed in a weird heat. We wound through three or four more twists in the road—that could have been dirt or gravel or some primitive pavement—before I tested out my newfound power: "There's a boogeyman around the next corner." My chest tightened and the whole car went silent as everyone leaned forward, twisting their heads to see... grass, grey rocks, bushes, the dark forest, and and and ...just things that didn't move. My brother laughed, and I felt naked—shrivelled—like someone had just drained the tub.

Wanting that sudden chill off my skin, my voice pale and skinny, I tried again. But no one hunched forward to see what was waiting. Disappointment. My brother Doug razzed me, then he started to give me advice about which kind of corner was best for boogeyman predictions. I was grateful my parents didn't call me a phoney. At the next bend, Joan screeched, "There's a boogeyman around...," like I had invented some kind of game she could play too. (Secretly, I was happy when no bear answered her voice.) Why hadn't I quit while I was ahead?

I can remember another day, drawing with waxy colours on slidey paper, down on the wooden floor inside of a rainy day, copying the shapes of letters. Not even trying to write out words, but somehow knowing how to spell my brother's name. Making the letters seen in books and from sounds in my head of loggers talking. Late in the afternoon, as I finished, Dad came in from work, his heavy wet white-grey coat above me. Something made me feel trapped by the page in front of me. Would he spank me? He leaned down, picked up the piece of paper, and read silently: DOUG IS A SHIT. Dad turned away, his mouth pulled open, strangely—trying to hide a grin. The novels I later wrote probably an unconscious search to join the two languages I heard as a kid: the "literary," educated, proper one that both my parents spoke and the "bad," direct, sometimes brutal one of the logging camp. Style for me, then, wasn't chosen but imposed—a hybrid of opposing Englishes.

At Port McNeill, there was a chopped-down wilderness right outside the only two rows of shacks. Bears in the early morning showed up in the backyard gardens, and it was a bit scary even to cross the one road to visit a friend (Brian?). Maybe he was six years old, spooning brown sugar—five, six, seven—onto his bowl of cereal. Didn't he care if his teeth fell out? After breakfast, Brian left the kitchen grinning and returned quickly with his dad's gun. The two of us walked out the back door, and I stood right beside him as he fired the rifle at a tin can on a stump. The noise filled and emptied my ears (and came again). I'd never before heard such loudness so near. Didn't show I was scared but pretended I had to go home right away.

Back then, running and running and running everywhere with my brother Doug, down on the crunchy beach, across the wide fields, out and back along the echoing planks that took us to the end of the pier, then circling back to the playground. The only time I got hurt was when I was high up in the air on a teeter-totter, and a bigger kid jumped off, banging my jaw-bone down on the iron handle. My face slippery with blood. While the first aid Doc stuck the split skin back together with thick adhesive tape, the strong smell of disinfectant that was like—and not exactly like—the sea distracted me. Mom worried that it would scar (it did).

I have no wish to skip over what's unremembered

and missing, but can't connect these episodic bits of memory into any fuller story shape. Am I trying too hard not to be seduced by narrative form? Without giving into that desire for an alluring story-telling shape, what's in it for a potential reader? On the Mississippi River, Melville's con artist hopes to fool the mark through an erotic rush of continuity, and, the listener, in a kind of wishful collusion, believes, allowing the teller of inventions to delude himself.

When I was five, a float plane took our family back down the coast, out of the wilderness. I went to kindergarten in westside Vancouver, far away from bears and noisy machines, then to grade one at Trafalgar School: concrete paths, neatly mown grass, a building shaped not out of wood but stone. One morning Miss Swanson handed back our spelling test. Pausing by my desk, she said, "Don't try to be funny." What did she mean? I glanced down at the list of twenty-five words I'd printed in pencil, each on its own line, and saw she'd circled an answer. I'd misspelled "ship" as "shit." I would never have had the nerve to do this on purpose—knew nothing of Freud back then. I was embarrassed, and confused about how this "bad" word had popped out of nowhere into this place of proper behaviour. Shame (or child-like cunning) kept me from speaking because I noticed I'd been given a perfect score. Miss Swanson thought I was joking. Humour must be a sort of success if it made up for a mistake. When I handed my grade one report card over to my parents, they studied its letters: "O" and "N" and "U." For that whole first year—in almost every subject—I received "N," for normal. But in all three of the behaviour categories,

I got "U," unsatisfactory. The only "O" was for art: outstanding. By grade two, I had learned to be dull (or just pretending?). In both behaviour and art, my designation was now "normal."

But that also could have been the year that I wrote my first book. Four pages long. I sat at at the oval kitchen table, banded in half-shiny metal, its hard surface flecked with dusty stars. My story told of a panda who was a cowboy called Curly who wore a red bandana who caught rustlers. Pictorially, there was no evidence of curliness. His solid, straight-furred form came from my weighty chunk of panda-shaped metal painted black and white that sat up and looked me in the eye. This kind of bear didn't live up the coast on Vancouver Island, but ate bamboo shoots—not flesh and berries like mine. I copied the plot-line of my story from a cowboy comic book, lifting the panda's speeches out of dialogue balloons. The picture boxes that I formed and filled floated together and apart, like the waves of the Pacific. Mom said it should be published. But I didn't make it up (I nearly replied), except for changing a cowboy into a gentle bear with a six-gun.

At Port McNeill, there had been a raw emptiness beyond the reach of culture. Dead trees in the constant logging trucks kept everyone remote. Yet along with the stench of a beached whale, dead and rolling on pebbles in the tide, there were words, and two parents who cared about us. Doug became a law partner; Joan, the head of a mental health team. Outside, back then, language was alive in that salt sea air, a second language that hid itself in curses and bad jokes and bare naming and loud laughter, breaking again and again, like waves against the wooden pilings of the wharf, telling of distant truths. Like everyone else, I was caught in the lottery of language, geography, and family. Now, getting off a Melbourne tram, this re-membering of fragments is like that small, far-ago comic book. But how else to piece together the unforgotten scraps of early childhood? Like Dad's scissored brown "scraps," his heterogeneous newspaper articles pasted into a semi-perishable "book."

Back at the Hotel Y, I make a phone call to Rev. Des Benfield, who, in response to my question about church records, states that my grandfather had not been a minister at Christ Church South Yarra. I ask him to check, please, under "curate." He's skeptical, but goes off anyway to look, and I'm beginning to doubt this is the right church. He picks up the phone and confirms that Rev. Ernest Reed Harrison worked at Christ Church—and was married there!

Jo and I take a tram down to Collins Street, and within ten minutes of entering the government building, I hold a copy of Ethel and Ernest's wedding certificate. A deeply upsetting document. Despite what I always believed to be true, my grandmother was *not* born in Australia, but, like Ernest, in England. No wonder I couldn't find her birth certificate here. Other curious details to consider later, but for now I carefully fold the wide sheet with its red star stamp and tuck it away in my rain-proof jacket—my connection to this vast and vibrant island and its "fair-go" people has been a delusion. I'm bereft.

While Jo heads off to the conical glass building and airy geodesic dome of the Melbourne Central

Shopping Centre, I wander into Dymocks Booksellers, bewildered that I am not who I am. Surrounded by so much Australian literature to savour and ingest that no longer belongs to me, I pick up Dorothy Porter's *the monkey's mask*, a prize-winning crime thriller in verse about a lesbian dick, that both Tess and Judith recommended. Hybrid forms, such as lyric narrative, may express a post-Empire space we Canadians share with Australians: an impulse to transgress old boundaries and loyalties. Its epigraph is a haiku by Basho: "Year after year / On the monkey's face / A monkey's mask." For a lifetime I've worn the face of Oz, now revealed to be a mask. I pay for the book, hide in my soft black briefcase the lurid cover of two naked coupling bodies, and hurry on towards the Victoria State Library.

Following up on my uncle's suggestion about the Australian Board of Missions, I quickly discover an entire journal. The first issue the library possesses is for 1915, and in May of that year is an article, "A WONDERFUL EASTERN CITY," by the Rev. E. R. Harrison. My Australian heritage has just vanished, but an ancestor suddenly jumps out. No personal letters from my grandfather survive, yet I'm now reading his century-ago words:

"One Sunday evening a friend and I walked to the top of Kurakakeyama, a mountain just behind Hakone, the village in which we are staying, and in the clear evening light we had before us one of the most wonderful views that I have ever seen. Looking round, we could see ten provinces, with wonderfully varied scenery, from flat plains covered with rice-fields to rugged mountain ranges which stood out boldly against the deepening shadows. At our feet the little village, with its sister village about a mile away, seemed to be nestling under the green mountain slopes by the side of a beautiful lake. Far in the distance the Pacific Ocean was sweeping into two big bays dotted with mountainous and wooded islands. Then as the sun was setting we looked towards the west, and, flushed with a golden glow, there stood out above everything the beautiful outline of Fujiyama, the highest and the most sacred mountain in all Japan, and deservedly one of the most famous in the world. Now the mists begin to collect in the valleys, and like fleeces of pure white wool they floated upwards towards the mountains, gradually blotting out the plains, the sea, the lake, and the mountains, and leaving us alone upon the mountain top with the memory of a very beautiful scene.

This letter gives me an uncanny sense of where my desire to travel and write came from. But as an outsider in matters of faith—in a contemporary world of Moslem terrorists and a born-again President threatening war—I flinch at my grandfather's last sentence about Japan's need for "the living Christ."

I flip through more bound pages, and there on the top right-hand corner for June 1, 1915, is a photograph of a man I'll never meet. Ernest wears a circling broad white collar and wire-frame glasses over friendly, luminous eyes.

I check my watch: don't wish to be a late guest. Tess has invited us to dinner this evening, partly so her daughter, Catherine, and Jo can talk about their work in film. Rapidly, I turn over more pages. Unreal, this sudden too muchness. Even as I'm speed-reading my grandfather's articles with joy and self-recognition (aside from the endings with their proselytizing fervor), time has run out on me. But I'm held by his vivid response to geography and curiosity about other cultures, the eye for the comical, his shifting of perspectives, descriptions which flare towards the poetic . . . an anticipatory echo of these travel jottings? Half-standing, I flash through more pages, conscious I really have to get out of this library right now—but I crouch here because on December 1, 1915 is something surreal for any son: news of his father's arrival in the world:

> "We rejoice to announce the birth of a son to the Rev. E. R. and Mrs. Harrison, missionaries in South Tokyo, on Sept. 28th. [In our family we always celebrated his birthday on the 27th?] We congratulate the happy parents, and we may assure them, on behalf of our readers, of our prayers and for God's blessing on their little one. We think we may now say, in a real sense, that we have three missionaries at work in Japan."

Outwardly, for much of his life, Dad was religious, but, later, less conspicuously so. I need to look again at the videotape interview of him in the ward as a dying patient. Might Dad have come to envy how fully Rev. E. R. Harrison lost himself in the light?

I frantically scan the back pages of the bound serial—deeper and deeper into the Great War, where Japan was England's ally—xeroxing as much as I can in the few minutes that I don't have left. The *Australian Board of Missions Review*, a bonanza. Not exactly the right metaphor, but, then again, the gold mines at Bendigo, Ballarat, and Castlemaine in the middle of the 19th century brought masses of people and enough wealth to Melbourne to support a violinist and a missionary. Heavily laden, I hurry away with all the golden words I've excavated.

Jo and I ride the commuter train to Malvern in Caulfield, where an attractive and personable young woman meets us in a familiar car: Tess's daughter, Catherine. She drives to their place and parks on the road because they're in the process of converting the garage into an in-fill house. We walk through the construction site into a house where books spill out into the dining room. With a hug from Tess in the kitchen, I feel at home. With last minute calls from her friends wanting to gather at a time of coming war, we're suddenly to be eight people for dinner. The only males are myself and Mortlock, the blackish terrier who at first is wary, then intimate. Carmella, a friend of Catherine's, has just come back from East Timor, and another Asian island that she's entered illegally to make a documentary film. I'm impressed by her nerve, idealism, and modesty. Anne-Marie, who's a bubbly, thoughtful, funny woman and the Arts Council Rep for Caulfield, arrives with some cleanskins wine (i.e., sold without labels), which turns out to be delicious. Finally, Judith Buckrich and her 13-year old daughter,

Laura, come in, completing the gathering. Tess is showing me a large book Judith has written, detailing the story of Melbourne as a working port, when Jo (who's been checking for e-mail) gives a shout. Canada will *not* be joining the war on Iraq!

I'm pretty astonished. Someone at the table has heard rumours of Arab refugees fleeing the US for Canada—like Vietnam draft-dodgers in the 60's? But Jo says there's no report of this on the net. Did the conspicuous earlier refusal of President Chirac and Québec's history of anti-conscription riots motivate our Prime Minister? Is it naïve to believe he only wanted to uphold the UN's stated goal of peace?

We're about to begin eating spaghetti when Tess proposes that we each hold up a dinner plate and have our picture taken. This odd domestic act feels playful and ceremonial—and a reminder of the world's rounded shape. The meal is festive despite the looming war, and discussion centres on tomorrow's demonstration. At this animated table, I'm interrupted more than once but it's fun fighting for conversational space, or just listening to these smart, engaged voices. With the laughter, good red wine, and zesty pasta, I travel back to Montréal, to the other side of the planet, where more than a decade ago friends like these became a substitute family in a city not of our birth, and dinners like this warmed many winter nights. In a Québec of FLQ bombings, political kidnappings, an assassination, an army tank outside our apartment window, and with the country I was born into fragmenting, I learned *joie de vivre* as a survival mechanism. Maybe Jo and I were, like many of those here, just young with idealism.

At the end of our Melbourne party, Tess asks her daughter to drive Jo and me to the train station. Sometimes I forget I was not yet 21 when I made the two significant decisions that gave my life a happy shape: to marry Jo and have children and to turn down U of T law school. Both irrational choices. We're riding in the car for quite awhile before Jo and I realize Catherine isn't heading for the commuter line: she's taking us all the way back to the Hotel Y.

Was it matter-of-fact help like this that initiated the fable of Ethel's birthplace? A family wishing to be Australian? I finger the ash that remains on the window ledge.

"Our Japanese Village" by Rev. E.R. Harrison

Australian Board of Missions Review, November 1, 1915

. . .

"The houses are just a big roof of thatch, smoke-blackened and grimy, with two side walls of wood and bamboo, and sliding screens back and front. All day long the wooden and the paper sliding screens are out of sight, and the washing, the cooking, the eating, the receiving of guests, and all the little doings which make up the daily round, the common task, are quite open to the public gaze. Then in the evening there are quaint little scenes in the lamplight—a professional story-teller entertaining a few of the village folk, or some sick person being pummelled and massaged back to health, or a picturesque group sitting on the floor round the little fires exchanging the gossip of the day, or perhaps the places are partly shut up and one can only see shadow-pictures on the paper *shoji*. But when the time comes to take out the padded quilts and 'go to bed' upon the thickly matted floor, then the outside wooden screens are slid into their places, and to make up for airiness of the daytime the houses are shut up like sardine-tins all night.

"The mountains around the village are covered with fir-trees, or bamboo canes, occasionally with sharp bamboo grass. The bamboo canes are in great request for making pipes and fans, and a hundred and one other things, and the grass makes a coarse kind of hay. There are wonderful wild flowers, the lilies being particularly magnificent. Some of the lilies measure over ten inches across, and we saw one stem bearing sixteen of these beautiful blooms. The butterflies are of all kinds, from tiny little blue ones which look like violets to handsome big 'bird butterflies' with velvety black or purple wings. In the evening the cicadas fill the air with their insistent stridulations, and if it is very warm the beautiful little fire-flies flit to and fro like wandering stars."

Thursday, March 20

In the rain, Jo and I get on tram #16 for St Kilda to check out a 1931 address that Gordon Sargood provided for "Miss Mercer," the then contact person, who probably was one of Ethel's sisters. We get off and hunt for 32 Charnwood Road. A swanky new building. Whatever structure was here in the thirties has been replaced. The high wall and iron gates add to my melancholy sense that the past is, despite the Faulknerian epigraph, mostly gone. I ask Jo to take a photo anyway: documenting failure? We walk onward, or backward, to 50 Barkly Street where Dad and Noel stayed in 1929 with their mother. A red-bricked, two-storey place with no distinguishing features whatsoever.

In the rain, we take the bus towards Christ Church in South Yarra, get off, and climb the steep hill towards a tall stone spire. Here, at the corner of Toorak and Punt Roads, my grandfather was a curate, met a parishioner, and was smitten. A bit tentatively, I enter the church whose ceiling of dark wood is relieved by a stained-glass skylight. As I approach the altar, a cloud passes by overhead. I turn and look back. A beautiful light filters through the overhead glass, falls as glowing air onto the empty wooden pews. Was Ernest's first vision of Ethel washed in this rose-red light?

For their marriage solemnized in the State of

Victoria, two quaint terms speak of social identities now defunct: *Bachelor* and *Spinster*. Their birthplaces, England: *St Ives* and *Croydon*. I probably should revisit St Ives, where Ernest had been one of seven brothers.

> As I was going to St Ives
> I met a man with seven wives
> Every wife had seven sacks,
> Every sack had seven cats,
> Every cat had seven kits.
> Kits, cats, sacks and wives,
> How many were going to St Ives?

Dad, who always tried to be truthful, said this nursery rhyme didn't come from his father's Cambridgeshire but from the more famous St Ives in Cornwall. In this Australian church, two wayfarers were joined together, *Clerk in Holy Orders* and *Violinist*. Music still must be a large part of church activities since a pamphlet lists a director, an organist, and an assistant organist.

For *Fathers' Rank or Profession*, the certificate for their marriage by banns according to the rites & ceremonies of the Church of England lists *Cattle-dealer* and *Civil Engineer*. Four heads of bulls make up the crest for his town of St Ives, where a big marketplace was established in the Middle Ages—after the bones of the obscure "Persian" Saint Ivo were discovered or misidentified on purpose there. Merchants from as far away as Ypres and Normandy sailed across the North Sea and up the Great Ouse River (which uncle Noel says is pronounced "ooze"). The chapel on its bridge on the road north from London once doubled as a tollgate.

In the back of this Melbourne church I pick up an envelope that reads, "Lenten Appeal 2003" and "Love the Lord your God with all your heart...." and "The Anglican Board of Mission—Australia Limited." Twice, I reach for my wallet to make a donation, but halt, conflicted—feeling like an imposter. But I keep the envelope. Ernest had ended up on the far side of the earth, a former reporter, a theology student from Cambridge University who had topped his class, a man no longer young still looking for what he might do with his life. The mission to Japan must have seemed like a godsend. Lingering by the open doorway, I browse through some folded, unstapled pages, and come across words from the Vicar: "Until war is justified or declared, I will talk and work for peace and disarmament. As a Christian I can do nothing less."

Jo and I go outside into the wet church grounds, and I half-intend to speak with Rev. Des Benfield. We stroll down a path in the garden which leads to a low building, a reception office where a woman with a broad smile greets us, offers tea, invites us to Sunday services, and smiles again, wonderfully. I'm totally mute. Unable to find a response. But Jo answers smoothly that we'll be on our way to Adelaide by then. Our distinct voices are at times interchangeable. I think of the poor, baffled real estate agent when we were looking for a place to buy, checking out dozens of houses over several days, and he expected to make the sale to the person who got into the passenger side of the front seat, the position of the decision-maker. But Jo and I kept (unconsciously) switching places with every stop. In the end, he didn't know who to make the pitch to. Were Ernest and Ethel,

57

like us, in having no one in charge of the relationship despite their age disparity: he, thirty-one; she, thirty-seven, at their wedding?

We walk west along Toorak Road, then turn right on a narrow road heading north towards the Royal Botanic Gardens. A man weeding his tidy lawn straightens up, greets Jo, "G'day"—the first time I've heard this Aussie expression outside of TV ads or Hollywood movies, and in the newly arrived sunshine it sounds both friendly and true. At the Observatory restaurant I order a slice of carrot cake and a flat white, which turns out to be a foam-less *café au lait*, yet I can't relax into a holiday mode because there's unmined research material waiting. Jo volunteers to come to the Victoria State Library to help with the xeroxing.

When we get there, people are passing out notices for the anti-war demo at 5 p.m. Inside the building, I discover the key first issues of the *A.B.M. Review* I borrowed yesterday but had no time to copy are unavailable, and may have been sent off to the bindery to be shrink-wrapped. Like the torture of Tantalus: the desired fruit visible on the branch overhead but just beyond the fingertips, and a crystalline stream at my feet which when I bend to drink turns to dust in my mouth. Replenishing my copy card, I begin to xerox excerpts from some later issues of the *A.B.M. Review.* At about 5:30 Jo goes outside to see if the demo's happening, and immediately comes back in for the camera. We both rush out to the broad, plaza-like space above the library's wide steps.

Four mounted police in shiny black helmets and bright yellow protective jackets sit astride black horses—a tail swishes at the neo-classical façade. The long faces of the four horses are sheathed from nostrils to ears in clear plastic masks. Below us, demonstrators in every direction fill the streets. People are perched on top of statues and in branches. Posters and placards in green letters read, "Don't Bomb Iraq," and depict John Howard's face with blood-red dollar signs. Next to Jo, a young man holds aloft one end of a banner that reads, "Arabs for Peace." Beside me, like caricatures of undercover cops, two beefy, balding guys with open blue windbreakers stand stiffly in front of the horses. From a small balcony on the building across the street, several storeys up, a young man speaks urgently into a microphone, and fists of protesters punch the air. The mounted policewomen on the far left horse stares ahead fixedly, her cheeks sucked in, but in this day's sunshine the mood feels unthreatening.

It could be Telegraph Avenue in Berkeley during the Vietnam War, except here in Melbourne there's no sporadic running ahead of the riot police, none of the festive rowdiness I remember, no tear gas, no half-bitter, half-humorous chanting, "Hey, hey / Ho Chi Minh / The NLF / Is gonna win"—and no risk of being deported to Canada. Back then, the combustible mood of peace protests mixed exhilaration and fear, perhaps echoing the manic dread of young American and Australian soldiers in the moments before combat. In Melbourne, at this adrenaline-free demo, a new speaker, a woman, calmly and lucidly sets out the crowd's concerns. I have to admire the way these protestors aren't fuelling up on the high octane of self-righteousness. For all the gestures of defiance, the tone in this immense gathering is *reflective*. Can't spot Tess, but I'm sure she's here somewhere. For no discernible reason, the four apocalyptic horsemen ride away—off to the building's side, leaving fresh dung by a Corinthian column.

I would like to linger in this shared brightness, but decide to return to my research. A woman librarian who's still on duty brings me the crucial first half dozen *A.B.M. Review*, having personally retrieved them from some obscure region. Many, many thanks. "Jottings from Japan." Jo comes in, reports the demo's continuing, though fairly sedately, and she helps me out again with the copying. I'm prepared to xerox until closing time, but Jo is getting restless, so we leave for some dinner, descending the library's now empty stairs, and walk over to the nearby Stalagtites. My research feels like the immobilized plaster dripping from the ceiling. After our meal, I come back to the Victoria State Library alone. I climb its marble stairway alongside an expensively dressed, carefully coiffed couple—the woman's high heels clattering. Their up-scale garb is a striking contrast to the t-shirts and running shoes of demonstrators here just a few hours ago. I copy and cut and staple what I hope are the relevant pages from several years of the *A.B.M. Review*. It's a semi-feverish activity that confers a satisfying, if false sense of orderliness—as though life were finite excerpts in folders instead of a continuous swirling away from summary and containment. But pages of print do make up much of the gettable past . . .

"Mrs. Harrison writes:-- "

The first words I've ever read from my father's

mother...and as I'm reading the words of Ethel *née* Mercer in this nearly deserted building, I hear the faint sound of a violin. Pulled out of the Australian research room to investigate the vibrations of these invisible strings, I find myself standing alone in a large vacant space with classical music wafting down an interior stairway. Puzzled and half-mesmerized, I listen to several bars, then return to my sliding-down pile of unxeroxed journals. But, mentally, I can't resume working, so I query the friendly librarian about this improbable, unseen music. She tells me there's a fashion show on upstairs—and I remember the couple hurrying up the outside steps in their stylish clothes.

Even into the late evening, when the whirs and hums of my machine quieten, I hear a violin.

Mrs. Harrison, a letter

Australian Board of Missions Review,
February 1, 1918

"We are to have four baptisms in a few days, and as I promised to be godmother to all the infants you will see that my responsibilities are rapidly increasing. We have lengthy 'go-dans' (consultations) over the names, many of the Bible names sounding very peculiar to a Japanese ear, and not easily translatable into their syllables. They have no 'L' and no 'Th' and no 'V' so one has to use a substitute. For instance Eva becomes 'Eba,' and if they want to say violin it becomes 'bayorin,' and so on. Some of the Old Testament names become quite unrecognisable under these transformations. The Japanese names themselves are most interesting; they are constantly coining new ones.

"One of our girls is called O Kan. She was born on Christmas Day, and it was very cold, so they called her O Kan which means 'great cold.' The other day we met a little girl whose name was Chiri. We asked the parents what it meant. They said, 'Why you know Chili is a long country and we want our little girl to have a long life, so we called her Chiri!' (Japanese for Chili)."

Friday, March 21

We mail books and blundies back to Canada, then, on this last day in Melbourne, revisit the Victoria State Library. Jo starts to scan and xerox the later issues while I stop to read more of my grandfather's prose: June 15, 1919. "Annual Report of Chiba District—Diocese of South Tokyo." July 7, 1919. "Social Conditions in Japan." My white-collar leftism has an ancestry. Like a muck-raking journalist, Ernest uses numbers to measure intolerable social conditions—and narrative as an implicit mode of protest. On January 7, 1920, there's a *cri de coeur* about the mission in Japan. In doubt, maybe despair, E. R. Harrison calls for radical reform, proposing a new missionary focus on industrial workers. Controversial these views must be, since the *A.B.M.* editor appends a reassuring note: "The Right Reverend the Bishop in South Tokyo has written to say in reference to the above article that it was sent to us with his full approval, and deals with a matter which he has himself urged from time to time in speech and writing, namely... that a Christianity not socially applied is not Christianity at all...." I agree with this sentiment, but need to hurry up...

"Up a Japanese Volcano." What's a missionary

doing climbing a hissing volcano in the dark for fun? An image of the human condition? As a Gemini, I like my grandfather's contradictions—his twinning of spirituality and physical adventure. I wonder what sign E. R. Harrison was born under, and if, as one literary theory proposes, I'm little more than an assemblage of pre-existing texts.

Temporarily, I ignore the next year of the *A.B.M. Review*, and instead grab off the library cart another book I've requested from the Main Catalogue, *Music in the cabbage garden: the pioneers of music in Victoria*, published in Melbourne, but the date's uncertain. I check the index in back, and feel let down when the name of Ethel Mercer is absent. However, several references are to Mr. Henry Curtis, the composer of her "Berceuse," leader of The Amateur Orchestra Society of Melbourne, and member of "The excellent String Quartet comprising Messrs. Weston, Curtis, Zerbini and Reimers, which could hardly be excelled in any part of the world." It sounds like absurd boosterism, but without being able to hear the quartet play, how will I ever know? There must be significant bits of musical history here, but not enough minutes to locate them. I could stay inside this building for another month, pressing pages face-down against the glass, but have agreed with Jo that in the afternoon on our final day in Melbourne we'll go on some kind of outing.

Such negotiations we do almost nonverbally. On this almost half-year journey, we're both smart enough to know we don't need the other one unhappy. While Jo's motoring through a later issue on my behalf, I again get distracted by November 7, 1920. "Congratulations

to Mr. and Mrs. Harrison on the birth of a daughter—
August 20th." Dad and Noel's sister, a figure of absence,
makes her appearance. Jo, who's levelled her height of
books, starts in on my glacially eroding escarpment.
Around noon, we complete the task, and I haul away
the weighty copies.

After lunch at the Victoria Market, we ride
the tram to Toorak: our destination is Como House.
Though made out of rendered rubble walls over two
feet thick, taken from the mudstone banks of the Yarra
which it overlooks, Como looks surprisingly summery.
Originally the hunting ground of the Woiworung
Aborigines, later a cattle run, the rural mansion
of Como was built in 1847 when Melbourne had a
population of only about 10,000 people. The two airy,
wide verandahs with spear-like railings are held up by
a dozen slender pillars, and as the low afternoon light
strikes the fresh paint, the white building appears to
tremble.

Inside, there is a ballroom of gracious proportions
where Nellie Melba once sang. Likely Ethel, before
she became a missionary's wife, played her violin in
this handsome room at some musical soirée—in a
performance marked by a depth of feeling and skillful
execution. The glittery chandelier repeats itself in two
ornately gilded oval mirrors set on a nearby wall. In
the corner of the room, roped off by a red velvet cord
strung between shining stanchions, is a grand piano,
its lid propped open. Like a racing car engine needing
one last quick adjustment before it accelerates off the
starting grid. This simile probably generated by my
sense of hurry and departure.

Jo and I have a quick meal at a 50's-style diner (lime soda, BLT, and fries), and are rushing to see *The Pianist*, but get sidetracked into Freedom, a kind of Aussie Ikea. Jo spots some colourful, inexpensive slip-on covers for our torn dining room chairs back home. However, by the time we can find someone to give our money to, the film's already started. Our last night is shaping up as an anti-climax. We decide to check out Lumière on Lonsdale St., but don't like our movie options, and walk back to the hotel and watch news on Iraq.

Jo, after a week here, is more than ready to move on. I, in contrast, can imagine making a life in this city. My connection to the land of Oz may only be a myth, but I refuse to be dispossessed of kangaroos, koalas, and kookaburras—one of whom woke me at Crunella Beach near dawn with its crying human voice. Melburn. Mel-bn. Melb-rn. Did Ernest and Ethel regret leaving Australia—as their sons did, in 1933?

Noel recalls,

As we moved further north each day we two would go to the stern of the vessel in the evening to sight the increasingly declining Southern Cross. Finally it was not there. That was a real wrench.

JOIE DE VIVRE IN HIROSHIMA

*. . . startled by a fresh, thick-crusted loaf of French
bread . . .*

Tuesday, April 15

Before boarding, Jo and I walk past a sealed-off lounge in which half a dozen doctors and nurses in blue plastic gowns and spacey headgear clutch thermometers in latex gloves, and publicly inspect several orifices of passengers deplaning. At Singapore, just past midnight, we board flight SQ998 for Japan, with mostly masked companions. This city-state has seen many recent deaths, so I'd argued for masks, saying we didn't know much about SARS, and (unfairly?) reminded Jo a similar virus had obliterated her father's lungs. One benefit of this scare is that after I lift the chair arms and stash the metal buckles, there are four vacant seats in the centre aisle to sleep across. Jo sits by a window, in her mask, reading, a row of three seats to herself. Waiting in my mask with its duck mouth for take-off, I have an irrational flash that with the SARS alarm I won't be allowed into Japan due to my vitiligo—harmless splashes of depigmentation on some of my tanned fingers.

My fatigued, too-busy brain ponders the film that Singapore Air showed on the flight from Australia, *8 Mile*, about Eminem. Inside my sweltering mask, I think about how in an America that refuses to acknowledge class, this iconic figure of angry paleness is both cool and white-hot with caste rage. (Go to sleep.) A knowing lostness burns through his rhymes.

If gangsta rap music with its hypermasculine bravado takes its origin in the seemingly irremediable black hole of slavery, then Eminem, the white dwarf from the trailer-park, somehow has edged his way into that too heavy darkness. (Go to sleep.) Narrating his own disappearance in the nighttime sky.

Hours later, a stewardess gently wakes me, instructs me to fasten my seatbelt. Trapped sweat dampens my face. Outside the cabin windows, a filmstrip of black sky. I loop one of the four belts diagonally over my hip, then stretch out again in unwary rest.

At Narita Airport, Jo and I take off our masks and drink several quick deep swigs of deliciously wet water. It's 7 a.m., and we're half-asleep, finding our way to the luggage carousel. I drop my carry-on into the top section of an empty trolley that's off to one side, and a Japanese man standing dozens of feet away says, calmly, "It's mine." I apologize, sensing this country must have an unusual culture of honesty. Despite potent drugs, my back is less than semi-good, so I will need Jo's help in lifting my big blue pack off the carousel. For months, the backpack has been almost a pal, but since last week it's turned into a burden. On the 75 foot ketch sailing us around the Whitsundays, I had leaned over abruptly in the middle of the night to turn off a toilet valve, then damaged myself further the next morning by jumping off the Iluka's high deck into the sunshiny sea and snorkelling madly around in what felt like an endless aquarium of bright fish. Jo assists me now in strapping the backpack onto a light wheelie contraption I bought in Brisbane, and we approach the passport control area. It's taken a lifetime to get this close…. As the woman in uniform takes the document I extend, her hair falls partway across her face like a sudden black rain. She smiles, and we roll on through.

Jo and I ride an elevator downstairs where we buy a phone card, then come back up to a vast indoor space that's totally empty, but has a bank of phones. Jo tries to call Pat de Volpi at work—we're supposed to ask for PA-TO-RI-KU DE BO-RU-PI—and we discover our newly purchased phone card doesn't work. Our one connection in Japan, *incommunicado*. But I'm too tired to care very much. Then a Japanese woman enters to use a nearby phone. When she finishes, Jo holds up the useless phone card and asks in English if the woman has any change. There's a quick nod that's almost a bow and then she runs full-tilt across the wide, unpeopled floor to the far side of the building where a shop is just opening up. In two minutes she's racing back, coins in hand, to exchange for our paper currency. Her flat-out sprinting, this energetic kindness to strangers, I just cannot believe. I try out my first word of Japanese, "*Arigato*...Thank you."

Exiting through a hallway, I find the men's washroom, but the door won't budge. Like some cartoon character at a pull door, I push again on the door's hard, smooth surface which has no handle to pull. A passing Asian man points to a round, stainless steel button on the wall. I depress it and the door swings magically open. Duh! Am I an idiot—and is this a country in love with the indirection of technology or what? A remoteness that erases from the physical act any apparent agent. Profoundly ironic, given Hiroshima and Nagasaki.

When I return to the huge, still nearly vacant

room, Jo is hanging up the phone, and collecting back coins. No answer from Pat de Volpi who'd e-mailed us in Australia to say that because he was working overnight at NHK, he'd meet us this morning in Tokyo's subway system. But there's no answer at either Japan's national broadcasting center or at his apartment. Uneasily, I'm reminded of a Rodney Dangerfield joke: "My girlfriend called me up, told me to come right over, no one was home. I went right over. No one was home." We ride an escalator down a floor to activate our Japan Rail pass, having heard a taxi ride from the airport into Tokyo costs $500 U.S. I ask the man in the JR office for the location of an internet site, but he doesn't understand the English question—and my Japanese is only a scattering of irrelevant phrases. The next train to Tokyo doesn't depart for over an hour, so we decide to go back up two floors to the main terminal in quest of a cyber connection, our only possible link to Pat who has invited us to stay in his apartment. He is cousin to one of my best friends, David de Volpi, the cinematographer, whose near-death from cancer largely motivated taking this trip around the world now. Against the far wall, I spot an internet site, and Jo e-mails Pat with "Meet us at head of train?" as the subject line.

We sit down for a few minutes, and I flip through the fat guidebook, learning a few more words of Japanese, but fatigue is upping my low-level anxiety. Jo and I decide to locate the boarding platform for the bullet train, the Shinkansen. We're directed to the head of a green trapezoidal train. Stepping inside the first car, I see that almost all of the dozen people here are Caucasian. For whose benefit is this segregation?

The conductor enters, halts at the front of the car, and bows, but aside from Jo and I, the seated passengers don't notice. I'm a little embarrassed, and hope this deferential gesture isn't restricted to this car of groggy *gaijins*, foreigners.

Accelerating smoothly, our streamlined train speeds past wet, surprisingly wooded countryside, and I'm too spellbound to know if we're moving at anywhere near the top speed of three hundred kilometres an hour. A grey mass of buildings appears, then, on top of a ridge, above what must be the city of Narita, a large, graceful temple. The motion is almost silent over the continuously welded tracks, and hypnotic. So different from the steam engine that hauled Canada into a country. The bullet train speeds on towards Chiba, where my grandparents lived and worked during The Great War and the rice riots that followed. In his 1919 "Annual Report of Chiba District," E.R. Harrison offers his perspective in the form of a paradox: he argues that dealing with pressing labour and social problems could be a way of working out the salvation of the Church. Given what Christian Europe had just done to itself in the mud and blood of trenches, might he be doubting the usefulness of that faith in Japan—if not the world? But I'm glad my grandfather sided with the wretched and the activists who were unwilling to postpone hopes for fairness until after the grave. A forerunner of liberation theology? Or am I fantasizing, creating an ancestor out of my own idealized self-image?

At Chiba, the train pauses: block after depressing grey block of slabs of apartments. In Canada, everything

Japanese I've encountered from sushi to kimonos to bonsai trees has been shaped into loveliness. I'm not prepared for all this industrial concrete in the rain. Do sheer numbers of people make for such desolation? My grandfather was an ardent missionary to these people's grandparents—to this underclass—but I'm no longer keen to visit Chiba. This journey that Jo and I have embarked on before it's too late has twin goals of fun and enlightenment, which here have become contradictory. I feel a nostalgic rush for the open continental space of Australia and want the train to move on. There are a few late-blooming trees, white and pink-blossomed, but mostly it's endless grim grey housing and makeshift shacks of broken wood lining the tracks.

We're moving once again, with Tokyo approaching fast: "A wonderful Eastern city," Ernest wrote. Soon there will be that charged moment of reckoning all travellers know when the tangible experience of a city displaces an imagined name. Outside now, in the wide rectangles of the train's windows, Tokyo begins to appear as it is: taller, brighter, newer, and more harmonious than the one in my mindscape.

At Shinjuku Station, Jo and I step off onto the platform—into a surging mass of ten thousand people—but have no idea which way to go. With me wheeling my backpack, we trail behind this amazingly quick-footed populace. We're pretty much lost. Then, astonishingly, there's Pat, looking fit, coming towards us! Jo hugs him, and, after a hesitation, he and I clasp briefly. Pat remarks that I no longer have a beard, which means we haven't seen each other for over a decade. Probably the last time the two of us spoke was in the Laurentians, north of Montréal, where a good-looking girlfriend of this handsome journalist would sunbathe topless on David's dock at Lac des Becsie. As Pat is about to lead us down a fairly steep set of stairs, Jo mentions my sore back and, although Pat is carrying a laptop, he slings my large backpack over a shoulder without a word. I hoist my empty wheelie thing in the air as a whimsical gesture of apology.

Edging past an up-rush of people, we descend the concrete steps in single file, then go around, through, out, and across to a subway station where Pat buys three tickets from a wall of bewildering machines—before Jo and I have even started looking for our yen. "Arigato." After a ride to Shibuya Station, we transfer to a private rail line, Tokyu Toyoko, that Pat tells us was put in by a department store to lure shoppers. As we're zooming along, he points out that part of a station's name, "yama," means "mountain." Its Chinese character, *kanji*, is like an E lying on its back, except that the middle stroke is longer, making a stylized hill. A few stops later, the three of us get off at Pat's station, Gakugai-Daigaku, whose kanji I cannot begin to puzzle out. Under a moist sky, I walk outside into the city of my dead father's beginning.

Oddly, the first thing I see, on the facing corner, is a French bakery. After this mild and literal disorientation, I'm struck by how everything on the narrow street—bikes, clothes, storefronts, faces—has a remarkable sheen. Despite the drizzle and press of people, nothing looks dirtied or torn, accidental, or forgotten. The shops sell the usual things, magazines and food, but, all around us, unknown words double as alluring images: the kanji transfigures the entire commercial block into the realm of aesthetics (an impression I never got in Chinese cities like Shanghai). Surrounded by all these shapely, enigmatic word images, I can only stare…like a Japanese tourist at Lake Louise in Canada's Rockies.

But soon my ear picks up an irritating, high-pitched voice. A huckster, outside a drugstore, manages to smile enormously and yell tirelessly into a megaphone at the same time. Money-making's overly familiar shrill shill ends my enchantment, and we walk on towards Pat's apartment. He explains that this district of Setagaya-ku was once a rural area west of Tokyo, known for its almonds. Even now, in every unpaved patch of earth, however squeezed, bisected, or shadowed by buildings, miniature gardens bloom. Jo asks Pat about the mysteries of Tokyo addresses, and he explains that a *chome*, roughly a two-block area, is assigned a number, and then given a numeral (or numerals) in front of the chome number to specify a particular building, but the buildings are *not* in numerical order because the system (used originally) follows the date of construction. At one street corner, the forepaws of an out-sized ceramic badger are about to beat on its drum-like belly, advertising a restaurant within. I half-remember a Japanese folk-tale about a hunter who spares a badger that then magically rewards him with both music and a feast. What more could humans want? After ten minutes by foot, we reach Pat's apartment block—opposite a coppery-domed, Chinese sea-food restaurant that he cheerfully describes as looking like "an atomic bomb."

We take the elevator to the 10th floor, and there I meet Fabiola (pronounced with a soft "v"), and her young daughter, Carlotta. They arrived just yesterday from their home in Torino, so in this Tokyo apartment three cultures blur as Pat switches from English into intermediate-level Italian to converse with Carlotta, his daughter, who's inherited his blonde hair and blue eyes. I worry that Jo and I are intruding on a family reunion of sorts, but the atmosphere's welcoming. We gratefully abandon our large packs in Pat's small office, then he leads us outside to the narrow front balcony, and points to where we might, if a scouring wind blows the smog away, glimpse Mount Fuji—Fuji-*yama*.

After relaxing a bit, Jo and I decide we should leave the (possibly newly reunited?) family trio some privacy, and begin exploring the city. Pat recommends the Meiji-jingu shrine, followed by a nearby walk along what he calls the Japanese *Champs-Elysée*, Omote-sando Boulevard. Carrying his sketch map, Jo and I find our way back to Gakugai-Daigaku Station, and stare at the wall where tickets are dispensed, trying to figure out numerals and kanji. A smartly dressed woman beside us glances over as we try to puzzle out the hieroglyphic options, then half-leans our way as we discuss destinations, coinage, and distances. Completing her purchase, she asks if we would like help. So much for the stereotype of the Japanese being too shy or too self-conscious about possible linguistic mistakes to talk with strangers. *Arigato.* Thank you. *Arigato gozaimus.* Thank you very much.

We catch a train back to Shibuya station, then with our JR pass get on the *Yama*-note line (which seems to circle a *hilly* section of Tokyo), and it's only one stop to Harajuku station, and the Meiji-jingu shrine. There's an impressive swoop to its wooden entrance gate, the *torii*, whose broad horizontal shape in the lower sky projects wide of the two supporting columns. This gateway structure has such grace that its enormous scale is felt rather than perceived. It curves upward like a splendid banner in the wind.

Jo and I stroll through the spacious park to the Shinto shrine itself, rebuilt in 1958 after Allied bombing destroyed the original. The *Lonely Planet* claims that "unlike so many of Japan's postwar reconstructions, it is altogether authentic." I wonder if my jottings, this attempt to reconstruct the past authentically, is caught in the same illusion? The structure of the Meiji-jingu shrine looks nearly the same as the one photographed by my grandfather for the *A.B.M. Review* in 1928, where he wrote about Shinto as

> "'the way of the gods'—the old Japanese religion, which deifies the forces of nature, fosters ancestor-worship, and particularly focuses the attention of the nation upon the emperors, living and dead. At the time of the Restoration in 1868 perhaps no force did more than Shintoism to concentrate the veneration and loyalty of the Japanese people upon the Emperor, and to weld the nation into one."

Jo and I pause on the steps of the shrine and read in a pamphlet that the "Date of Establishment" for this structure is "1st November, 1920"—as if the shrine's total destruction in World War II and its subsequent rebuilding never happened. The pamphlet also makes an inadvertent pun about the enshrined souls, Emperor Meiji and His Consort, Empress Shoken: "Japanese cypress wood from Kiso, the best lumber produced in Japan, is solely used." Above the round supporting posts, the lilting rooflines sing out under the dark-grey sky.

We enter the fairly modest inner courtyard, whose spatial harmony gives a sense of unhurried fullness. We visit the Meiji-jingu-neien, the adjoining gardens. Even in the drizzle, it's a simple pleasure to be walking around without a pack. Some blossoms are out, but most plants have only buds. The irises, the garden's main attraction, are just wavy green shoots in a sea of mud **and** will fully flower only in June. On the long, curving, intersecting footpaths, we encounter only two people. Wet but far from unhappy, we follow the broad pavement back under the torii, out of the park, and into the urban millions.

Along the Japanese Champs-Elysée, a tall colourful building off to our right is called Condomania—a phallic tower devoted to birth control? The Omote-sando Boulevard itself is bordered by smart bistros, expensive-looking boutiques, and chic outdoor cafés. We turn right at Aoyama-dori, and walk past the UN university and a shop whose window displays colourful butterfly nets. It's hard to imagine anywhere else in the world that would have a store for lepidopterists. A hemmed-in street leads us to Shibuya Station, from which we easily retrace our way back to Pat's, where Fabiola has made everyone a tomato pasta, with a fresh tofu that's been lightly fried, along with some zesty spinach. My only contribution to supper is tall, white, black-starred cans of Sapporo beer.

Later, when Jo and I stretch out for the night in Pat's small office on a thin foam, I'm aware that Pat and Fabiola who've been living apart on different continents for several years will tonight be sharing the one bedroom with their daughter. Accommodating us. I realize, as well, that Italy and France have been significant references for this first day in Japan. A wonderful Eastern-Western city? And—not exactly an epiphany—the joy of sharing an (almost) family meal in a faraway place outweighs the pleasure of the sightseeing in this city of resurrection and mirage.

"Jottings from Japan" by Rev. E.R. Harrison

Australian Board of Missions Review, July 1, 1917

"The Japanese countryside is always more or less green, for when other trees have shed their leaves there is still left the varied foliage of an abundant supply of pines, firs, and cryptomerias. But the muddy wastes of the rice fields are rather desolate-looking in the winter, and I was glad to see the green crops springing up, with patches of brilliant yellow rape, and here and there on the hill sides and in the villages the bright pink of the budding peach trees, or the more delicate shades of cloud-like cherry blossoms. In many of the rice fields men and women were up to their knees in mud and water digging away with heavy rake-like forks, or building up the low mud walls which separate the different fields. Occasionally a powerful looking ox or a horse would be pulling a very primitive plough, but most of the work in Japan is done by hand.

"A couple of snakes by the roadside would have caused most Australians to get busy with a big stick, but I let them glide away untouched. For one thing they were quite harmless, and for another Japanese people are not of the snake-killing variety. About a month ago some coolies were working near a reservoir in an outlying suburb of Tokyo when they came across a whole colony of snakes of various kinds. At first they fled in terror, but afterwards they returned and captured some three hundred of the reptiles in bags. They talked of killing them, but the local inhabitants raised such an agitation, being convinced that the snakes were messengers of Kwannon, the goddess of mercy, that finally the whole lot were returned to their native haunts.

"A foreigner is naturally a source of interest to the country folk, but as a rule they are quite polite. A man's foreign clothes are so common, being worn by railway officials, school teachers, soldiers, and so on, that they pass without any attention. But when my wife goes in to the country, her dress, and particularly the hat, is always commented upon. Nearly all remark upon my height, whilst the size of my nose—which is quite inconspicuous as British noses go—impresses some. Various guesses are made about my nationality. The children are content to pass me as 'Mr. Stranger,' or 'Western Ocean man,' or occasionally, 'Aboriginal.' Some of the grown-ups, who of course know more about it, say that I am a *Shinajin*, or China man. One man, for some unknown reason, thought I must be Korean. But the worst of all are the wretched people who will persist in regarding me as a German spy. In the Japanese way of saying them, 'Australian' and 'Austrian' sound very much alike, and some people cannot get it out of their heads that I am an emissary of the Central Powers. When we moved from Tokyo to Shizuoka, a Japanese newspaper published a paragraph headed, 'Is the suspicious stranger a German spy?' They said I had suddenly disappeared with a trunk and my wife and child, and that the police were searching for me without success. However they paid me the compliment of saying that I spoke English very well."

Wednesday, April 16

A hot day as Jo and I start off late for the Edo-Tokyo Museum—Pat has been there twice. At Gakugai-Daigaku Station we realize there's a button to push on the ticket dispenser to get English. Pat's instructions are to wait for a silver train that *doesn't* stop at the head of the platform, then ride the Hibiya subway line to Akahabara, there transfer to the Subo line, and get off two stations later at Ryogoku. We arrive at this last station, and walk outside into the sun, stopping by the white stone sculpture of two wrestlers in front of the Sumo Arena, their bums darkened by the sweat of countless caresses.

At the stadium-sized Edo-Tokyo Museum, after riding up an extremely long escalator, Jo and I walk *over* the first exhibit: a full-scale replica of the Nihonbashi Bridge. Historically, distances in Japan were measured from the foot of this bridge, whose rebuilt structure in its gleaming newness is strikingly inauthentic. This arched, diagonal presence separates the museum's reconstructed pasts of this two-phased city: Edo to our left, Tokyo to our right; the shoguns, then the emperors. The original bridge was built at the start of the Edo period, 1603—the year (which I recognize as a Shakespeare prof) that King James VI came down from Scotland to succeed Queen Elizabeth on the throne of England.

The museum's guidebook quotes Hayashi Shihei as saying that the water passing under the Nihonbashi Bridge flows to London. And, in fact, these connecting seas brought Ernest and Ethel, by indirection, from England to Japan. Striking parallels, too, exist between these two temperate island nations that for much of modern history have dominated the salt water, and their respective continents.

Beginning with the origins of Edo as a fishing village, the museum shows its expansion into the gold and lacquered city presented on folding screens: castles, shrines, and samurai residences. Even the Great Meireki Fire (1657) didn't slow down the pleasure-seeking of the *daimyos* (or lords), and of their warriors who were obligated to be in residence at Edo. Recreated here in what feels like a film set are their amusements: a reconstructed kabuki theatre inn, a towering moveable shrine used in processions, and the elegant clothing of samurai and geishas. Jo and I pause at a storefront displaying the multiple steps of coloured woodblock printing, *ukiyo-e*. The museum's guidebook asserts that "the lower wrungs (*sic*) of society in Edo benefited from the economic trickle-down." In the Edo-period bookstore I read of *kibyoshi*, popular satirical novels written in the *hiragana* syllabary instead of the more complicated kanji characters, and wonder if one of Dad's favorite expressions, "to put the kibosh on something," derives from his Japanese past.

Jo and I cross over to the Tokyo section of the museum, where the Bricktown exhibit depicts the process of Westernization. This British-designed cluster of brick buildings in the Ginza area replaced the traditional wood structures that fires incinerated. The male manikins here wear European suits, and their former top-knots are severed. In one ghostly display, there is only a linked-chain pocket watch, a brass-locked briefcase, and a detachable stiff white collar, using only a few props to show how the modern fuses with the western—with a tinge of retrospective humour? My interest quickens when we reach a simulated household from the era that Ernest and Ethel lived in Japan. Did they turn on electric lights like those, sit on such chairs, hear voices or music from Melbourne or London on a crystal radio set like that one? My appetite for insignificant details from the past grows keener with my aging—perhaps I'm hoping a deeper sense of personal history will compensate for a shrinking future. This trip's foraging after what has passed away links understanding with pleasure, but also is shadowed by a fear of too lateness.

Here now are relics that survived the five massive Allied bombing raids which flattened most of Tokyo. For balance (or implied causation?), the museum displays the parachute bombs with which the Japanese planned to terrorize North America. Overall, the museum's near-geological exhibition tells how the people of Edo-Tokyo have again and again layered over obliteration with re-creation. After all the earthquakes, fires, tsunamis, volcanic eruptions, typhoons, and repeated aerial raids that left no further military targets, re-building became the city's identity. Time for Tokyo is not continuous but interruptive. From each disaster, a new historical past emerges, one that's assimilated to a much longer rhythm of re-making. And in this huge hall full of physical replicas, I glimpse a possible truth: this city itself is a kind of splendid and honest fake. The logically separable categories of old and new, which North American cities understand as a choice between preservation and change, blur here. When the two of us leave the museum, I'm at least half in love with the polished wood of the Nihonbashi Bridge beneath my running shoes. This shiny life-size model isn't—yet is— the real connective shape which measures the repeated explosions of new forms blossoming as Edo-Tokyo.

On our way back to Pat's, I suggest we check out Electric Town. At Akahabara Station, Jo and I get off the train, only to be overwhelmed by blocks of high towers of glass displaying electronic stuff for sale in every window at every level. Thinking maybe I can get a deal on a laptop computer, we go into L'Aox and ride an elevator up several floors, but somehow we get off at household goods. I find myself staring at an egg-shaped vacuum cleaner, apricot and pale-aqua in colour, wondering if it, too, will eventually end up on show inside the Edo-Tokyo Museum. After a few minutes, it's clear both Jo and I have already looked at too much today.

So, returning to Akahabara Station, we find our way to the Hibiya line, and get caught in a squeeze of too many people. Jo and I lock onto each other's eyes and, in sync, dart on board. I bump my head on a hanging ad in the middle of the subway car, and realize at six feet I'm the tallest person in sight. At Naka-meguro the train halts, and we have to disembark. Jo and I stand on the platform, trying to sort out what to do next, when someone hits me from behind on the shoulder. I turn, adrenaline coursing through my body, and face this burly guy who demands gruffly, "Where you want to go?" I'm dumb (in both senses of the word), but Jo is quick to answer, "Gakugai-Daigaku." This middle-aged Japanese man with a brush-cut and a working-class American accent says, "Don't take this train. The next one," then he turns away. Exactly the opposite of the stereotype: helpful and brusque. With twenty-five million people in Greater Tokyo—nearly the total population of Canada—there's little room for random violence in Japan. Considerateness must be learned as part of group survival.

At Pat's, another Japanese-Italian combo for dinner: miso soup and butterfly pasta. Fabiola tells us that on her first trip to Tokyo she was having a drink with some Japanese women friends who toasted her, "Kompai," and, when she raised her glass and gave the traditional Italian cheer, "Chin chin," they covered their mouths to hide their laughter. Apparently, "chin chin" in Japanese sounds like "penis." Pat asks about our visit to the museum and I mention the devastation of Tokyo by Allied bombing. He says only the poorer part of the city was destroyed, intentionally, as the Americans planned to stay in the better districts as occupiers. After dinner, there's some domestic weather when Carlotta loses her toy hamster behind the bathtub, and temporarily becomes distraught. I do the dishes and realize that after months of hostels and hotels I've missed the human friction of non-tourist lives. Later, as Jo and I bathe together in the sit-up tub, I reckon Pat will have a hard time getting rid of us—but the invitation was only for a couple of days.

Thursday, April 17

"Play it by ear," Pat says, when I ask him about the duration of our stay. We've already planned—via a day trip away from Tokyo—to give them a break from us.

Using our JR passes, Jo and I catch a bullet train rushing east towards Yokohama, then on to Kamakura. On board, we're the only gaijins in sight. We rough out the day's itinerary, foregoing the famous Kamakura Daibutsu, a huge bronze statue of the Buddha. Forking paths impose such tough choices on the traveller, mingling anticipative pleasure with a pricking sense of loss. But the small Zen monasteries we're headed for hold out the promise of quiet greenness.

At Kita-Kamakura Station we leave the train, walk beside the tracks, and enter Engaku-ji, the first Buddhist shrine of the day. The site is steep, with enclosing hills and an up-and-down terrain, so almost every step provides a new perspective on the white and pink flowers, the Japanese maples, and the varied greens of the conifers. A monk in dark blue wears what looks like a woman's pale summer hat, its wide band knotted into a bow, while a long white flap of cloth hangs from each side of the hat as shelter from the rain or today's sun—and from intrusive tourists watching as he snatches up stray garden bits and tosses them into the round bamboo basket strapped to his back.

We cross over the railway tracks to Tokei-ji, which was once a female monastery. Again, we climb up, through steep, well-tended gardens, and near the top of this hillside, Jo and I sit down among the gravestones. We unbag juice and cheese and French bread. Eating beside the departed feels oddly comfortable, but when a quartet of Japanese visitors approaches, I think this picnicking might be disrespectful, and tuck away my lunch. Nuns no longer live here but in the past a woman who resided three years in Tokei-ji could obtain a divorce. A psychological resonance between these garden sites of retreat and Japan's long, self-chosen withdrawal from the world?

Back onto the roadway, we continue our descent towards the city of Kamakura, strolling past a wall of drink machines: I can't believe the unappetizing name on a can, "Pocari Sweat." At Jochi-ji, we find a neat garden nestled in a cypress wood, but it is without topographical surprises—and the buildings themselves, which post-date a 1923 earthquake, lack zen-ness. The most intriguing feature is the three wooden statues enthroned on the central altar, all with large halos. Amida on the left representing the past, Shaka (or the Gautama Buddha) embodying the present, and Miroku, who will only appear five thousand years after Shaka's arrival in Nirvana, signifying the future. Shaka dominates, seated in the middle with the highest halo, but judging by the relative heights of Amida and Miroku, the past is less important than the future— doing in another Western cliché about Asian sensibility.

Walking parallel to the railroad tracks, Jo and I arrive at what *Lonely Planet* calls "Kamakura's most important Zen temple," Kencho-ji. Guys in white hardhats with power saws renovate (or newly construct?) the entrance gate as well as some big wooden buildings. It's like we're back in the Edo-Tokyo Museum, except it now feels as if we're looking at a copy of something that has no original. Monstrous tour buses disgorge loud-chattering people, their video cameras whirring, denying this monastery any tone of contemplation. One shaven monk arrives in a glossy black car like a top party official in China, and I recall the opening lines of Wordsworth's sonnet: "The world is too much with us; late and soon, / Getting and spending, we lay waste our powers." Across the roadway is the Enno-ji temple, whose statues depict the judges of hell—their fierce faces seeming to stare at the Kencho-ji temple in righteous anger.

Close by these two Buddhist sites is Kamakura's main Shinto temple, Tsurugaoka Hachiman-gu. Its red torii is impressive, and on the spacious paved grounds under the pink blossoms of trees kids run freely, but the main building is under repair, scaffolded off. We walk on, downhill, into the city itself, with the ocean appearing on our left. Kamakura, the capital of Japan before Kyoto and Tokyo, now has the pleasantness of a fairly quiet seaside town. We peer into smart shops, and stop to buy ice cream cones: mine vanilla, Jo's sweet potato, which is purple in colour.

Outside again, we're following the sidewalk that slopes gradually to sea level when I hear a beating whoosh, and a huge grey-white bird with a wingspan of at least five feet barely clears my left shoulder and Jo cries out. The bird has attacked her! Her ice cream cone has splashed onto the pavement, and there's a small cut on the middle finger of her left hand. I turn to see if it's coming back, but no threat is visible in the nearby air. Jo says she's not hurt—was just unpeeling the wrapper at the bottom of her cone. High above the bay, several dirty-white birds circle in the soft breeze. Jo, with her oblique humour, quips that in Japan you're not supposed to eat food on the streets. She thinks the bird was attracted by the ice cream, but why did it fly right past me?

I speculate that her wedding ring caught its eye, as in stories of magpies and ravens, and see again in my mind Whitehaven Beach in Australia where we walked down a boardwalk to a radiant turquoise sea and stepped onto the whitest sand *ever*. It actually squeaked. Jo, the optometrist's daughter, recognized it as pure silica, the material that when heated was used in the lab to adjust frames. She took off her marriage band and rubbed it in the white white sand, and within seconds, the wide gold band glittered and gleamed as brightly as when I bought it decades ago. A fairy-tale transformation, and now that other-worldly shine might explain the blood on my wife's finger.

Jo is unfazed by this sudden, violent encounter with nature, but we decide to take the train back to Tokyo and the sanity of urban life. On board, I find myself staring at an ad: a handsome, well-dressed Caucasian guy is handcuffed to a pretty Japanese woman. Unable to read the text, I can only guess at what's being sold. Then I notice how every young woman, and many of the men in our rail car, have dyed their beautiful black hair an acid chestnut. Why does the West have such appeal? Perhaps it's just wanting to see someone else in the mirror, like me on this trip?

Over sushi supper, Pat refuses to believe our story about the bird attack. Even after Jo shows him the red cut-line on the finger of her left hand, he's unconvinced—a skeptical news guy. I narrate my theory involving silica and shininess, which I'm probably too fond of because it causally links Australia to Japan. When I ask Fabiola and Pat about the train's poster of the handcuffed couple, he laughs, explaining it is an ad for private English language classes. How to take our tongue prisoner?

"The Japanese Prayer Book" by Rev. E.R. Harrison

Australian Board of Missions Review, September 1, 1917

"One is inclined to agree with the old Jesuit missionary who declared that the system of writing in use in this country was evidently 'the invention of a conciliabule of the demons to harass the faithful.' Of course one doesn't mind beginning at the wrong end of the book, and reading from top to bottom instead of left to right. When you get used to that way of reading it is just as good as any other. But when you get the strange enough sounds of the Japanese language set forth in that deservedly unique system of hieroglyphics known as Chinese characters, you feel that you have a legitimate source of grievance.

Greek looks rather strange to English eyes, Hebrew looks stranger, but both are mere child's play compared with that brain-racking system which can produce a dictionary of some 88,000 characters, containing anything from one to about thirty strokes each, and be ready to go on until further orders. However, with regard to these so-called 'word pictures'—the picture part of which generally existed only in the fertile imagination of some old Chinese scholar of bygone centuries, and has long since died a natural death in the perpetual struggle of dots and dashes v. time and convenience—it is mercifully fortunate that the knowledge of a few thousand of them will carry you a long way towards a practical use of the written language.

"But when you think that you are out of the wood, you find that one of these characters may be called by a variety of sounds, and you have to learn how and when these various sounds ought to be used. To make matters still more complicated—I had almost written interesting—the grammar and words of the written language are very different from those of the colloquial, and it almost seems that you overcome one difficulty only for the sake of being confronted with another. So perhaps you can understand that sometimes, when our eyes are tired and our brains weary, we sadly recall the words of the student from across the Pacific, 'Wal, I guess we shouldn't be doing all this if it hadn't been for that Tower of Babel stunt!' E.R.H."

Friday, April 18

Almost like commuters, Jo and I ride the subway system to Oeno Park, where the first thing to strike my eye is an unexpected work of art: a manhole cover. Instead of a round featureless thunk of metal, this disk offers a raised design of cherry blossoms of such lyricism that I hesitate to step on it. In North America, with its residual Puritanism, aesthetic delight is either quarantined off or used to sell things. In Japan, the pleasing and the functional are joined as one.

We walk past blue tarps and tents that are neatly folded and stacked on the lawn of this very upscale park with its imposing cluster of museums. Every evening, people who fall into the uneasy socio-economic category of the working homeless unfold and raise this camping gear. This morning, standing by some slender trees, are a few individuals who might have slept the night here. It's remarkable that officials allow this showcase locale to be the ongoing site for temporary shelter. Disturbing that many with jobs in Tokyo can't afford to rent even the tiniest apartment. When Jo and I flew out of Vancouver months ago, the headlines blared of the forced removal of squatters occupying the old Woodward's department store—their faces mostly imaged as the unemployed and unemployable in a Downtown Eastside long associated with drugs and distress. At Oeno Park, the carefully folded tents share the groomed landscape with the grand Tokyo National Museum. In this accommodation of the city's homeless workers in a preeminent place of national pride, the Japanese show themselves to be more concerned with looking after others than with presenting a pristine image. But, likely, what's symbolized by these blue tents is the world's even more inegalitarian future.

In the first room of the Tokyo National Museum, Jo and I spend half an hour by ourselves, mesmerized by the pottery: how can clay and bone be fired with such useful beauty? A professorial American comes in, eager to talk to fellow foreigners—luckily, his talk about Japanese ceramics is engaging and full of space for dialogue. The conversation veers to Frank Lloyd Wright's Imperial Hotel, and he mentions that its architectural remnants are kept at a location not far from here. Will we have time to check these out?

In the next room, Jo studies the kimonos avidly, responding to the design choices as a fibre artist, one of her many overlapping sequences of selves: model, mother, ACTRA member, published psychologist, dancer with wounded knees, fashion buyer, print editor, film producer, community organizer, and the wife who doesn't want to be written about. I can only half-sense how the details of sewing interact with colours, textures, and forms. By the time we complete the circuit of the museum's first floor, we're hungry for lunch: some delicious hunks of bread we've brought and cans of lemonade that we buy. Afterwards, we ascend to the second floor where the lacquer ware (which usually bores the shit out of me) seizes me with its otherworldly glow. It's as if these shapely black objects have somehow absorbed the moonlight. What was in that machine drink? It's only in the museum's final rooms, staring at walls of Westernized painting, that I get dulled out.

Outside once more, I suggest we go across the spacious grounds to another splendid building. Inside this one is a 12th century poetry anthology on display, a work from the Heian Period. Fine paper-making and calligraphy, but, unlike my grandfather, I can't read a single word. In my illiteracy, this vertically-ordered shaping of exquisite, many-stroked characters is a little crazy-making. Dozens of Japanese men—and several women—press in close to this medieval book, taking extensive notes. This handwritten work must be as important for Japanese literature as Chaucer's *Canterbury Tales* is for the English tradition. Likely, these heavy-duty scholars will come back tomorrow since the pages of the manuscript are turned each day according to a posted rotation. From their hushed intensity, I intuit how much I'm missing out on.

After taking the subway to Tokyo Station, we set off for the East Gate of the Imperial Gardens. The low light bounces cherry-blossom pinks, deciduous yellow-greens, and dark conifer greens off the slightly rippled surface of the large waterway, giving to each wet colour shape a washboard effect. On the far side of the wide boulevard, I spot the Imperial Hotel, in its third incarnation. Rather than this prosaic building, I dream of Frank Lloyd Wright's pyramidal form that kept floating upright on the mud when the great earthquake hit. Now it is stored away in pieces instead of looming skyward, like a huge pagoda—or like Mount Fuji itself—two of the suggested models for the Imperial Hotel. Leaving the expansive Imperial Gardens, and walking for a block or two, Jo and I are surprised to see the Victorian façade of the railway station. Then realize, in seconds, it's ersatz. Like most of the city, this has been rebuilt after the Allied bombing, but without the winking irony of a post-modernist sensibility. Nearby, four overhanging cranes jerk speedily upwards an unfinished office tower. In this rush to the new, yesterday doesn't seem to haunt Tokyo. It's as if the present is engaged in a friendly, long-distance conversation with the past, one in which grandparents at the other end of the line talk to offspring who must construct newly as they had to.

And in this place of his bicultural beginnings, I think of my father, and especially of his article on Frank Lloyd Wright's Japanese architecture. It may hold a life lesson about keeping your footing in a muddied, shearing world. John Robert Harrison wrote his newspaper parable before I was born, at the start of another war.

Back at the apartment, Pat mentions that a man he barely knew rushed over at work, shook his hand, and congratulated Canada on not invading Iraq.

"When Disaster Hit Tokio" by John Harrison

The Hamilton Spectator, Monday, October 23, 1939

"The most interesting fact observed was that buildings made of reinforced concrete stood up the best to the shocks. The most outstanding example of this was the Imperial hotel, built by the famous American architect, Frank Lloyd Wright. Wright had studied conditions in Japan and when he was commissioned to design the new hotel he decided to construct an earthquake-proof building, if that were possible. Reinforced concrete, he determined, was the only material which would create such a structure, but this alone was not sufficient. At a certain depth beneath the hard surface rock he discovered that there lay a strata of soft ground, almost swampy. With great daring and ingenuity he ordered the workmen to dig down to this soft strata for the foundations, flying in the face of all previous experience by not placing the basis of a building on firm ground. His theory was that if the pillars which were to support the building were embedded in resilient material, the effect of a shock would be minimized, for the soft earth would act as a shock absorber. When the earthquake took place he lived on tenterhooks for a few days, not knowing whether his theory had held water, for all cable communications were cut off for a while. Some days after the disaster he received word from the government that his idea had been sound and that the hotel had withstood the shocks, affording a temporary home for thousands."

. . .

[At the bottom of this newspaper clipping, my father has printed in capital letters, "AD MATREM MEAM," which I would translate as "To My Mother." The strong emotion he felt towards his birthplace is also made clear by a note he has added in a written hand, "I wish they wouldn't botch it up."]

Saturday, April 19

At 6 a.m. Pat wakes us up, says Mount Fuji is visible from his small balcony. Jo and I struggle up to find a strong wind has blown away the grey smog that usually hides the famous volcano. This white-topped splendour of nature looms above the miles of concrete apartments, so it's sort of worth getting up this early. I remember hearing as a kid that my grandfather died skiing down it. Noel laughed at this story, saying, "I love that—we shouldn't let that one die." Only half-awake, Jo and I head back to our sleeping mat in Pat's office, but there he is, seated at his desk, back to us, hitting keys on his plugged-in computer. I have to grin at the clever, not ungenerous way he's freed up his needed work-space. I pull our camera out of the pack and return to the balcony to shoot Mount Fuji, but before I can compose a shot, in drifts a grey-white smog that obscures the sacred mountain.

It's our last full day in Tokyo. Jo and I decide to take an early morning walk to see the neighbourhood of Setagaya-ku. She is excited because tomorrow Jennifer, the daughter of her closest childhood friend, is going to travel with us to Takayama in the Japanese Alps. Given my wife's holiday mood, my research feels postponable. A little girl on a bike passes, a white fluffy dog riding in her front basket. We go a few more blocks, locate a post office, but it is shut. However, a nearby shrine, with high surrounding walls, has its wide wooden gate ajar, revealing a seductive green garden. Jo and I go several paces inside, but then, unsure of our welcome, return to the street. Around the corner, in a small park, young children play happily: no adults in sight. How can 3- and 4-year old kids be left unattended in Tokyo with no sense of neglect?

The shops around Gakugai-Daigaku station are pretty quiet, but an optometrist is open. We enter and I mutely hold out my glasses with a loose lens. Delicately grasping the frames, a smiling woman hurries away with them into the backroom. In blurry focus, my eyes note the uncluttered design of this space that somehow manages to display elegantly hundreds of pairs of glasses. A few minutes later, the woman comes back, hands me my glasses with a screw tightened (or glued), both lenses cleaned, a slight bulge on the left earpiece straightened out, and refuses any payment. "Arigato. Arigato gozaimasu."

We return to the apartment and set out for lunch with Pat and Fabiola and their daughter. Carlotta wears a new purchase: pink rainwear with small white polka dots and a hood with two large rabbit ears. In the window of the restaurant Fabiola has picked out, I look over the sculptures of the food on offer. Inside, Jo orders *unagi*, the eel, while I choose steak strips in soup with the ropey noodles favoured by sumo wrestlers. Pat mentions that a guy at work thinks the bird that attacked Jo at Kamakura was a kite. While I await my noodle soup and steak, my brain sizzles with the phrase, "detested kite," an insult in *King Lear*. Fabiola is going off on a week-long side-trip with Carlotta and two Japanese friends, so no grand romantic union with Pat is in the cards, but everyone's comfortable as Jo sets her camera on a ledge and all five of us grin for a picture. I lean in with my left elbow on the table, Pat in a black t-shirt rests his chin on a hand, Fabiola lifts her oval head above her daughter's round face, Jo with her purple top flings herself back onto the bench just before the flash goes off, while Carlotta, who has bent her dark-blonde head towards the table's centre, holds up a palm with quizzically spread fingers. It feels like a farewell. Fabiola tells me her mother is a translator, and invites us to stay with her and Carlotta in Italy when we get there.

After lunch, Jo proposes that the two of us go to the Kabuki-za. For 900 yen each, from high up on the fourth floor, we watch a very stylized play. On the extremely wide stage below us with its cinemascope breadth are thirty-two actors. I like how at some of the entrances and exits a few people in the audience shout out the names of the actors. By breaking the performance frame in this way, these knowing fans, paradoxically, make me more alert to the next dramatic moment. The play itself is quite followable despite the high male voices speaking an unknown tongue in a simulated gender. What's theatricalized here in vibrant costumes and piercing voices, love and violence—and attendant issues of loyalty and honour—is more basic than language. But I'm not sure if I'm fascinated or bored (why else count the number of actors?).

That evening, Pat shows us an un-cropped photo from the internet of angry Iraqis pulling down an enormous statue of Saddam Hussein in Baghdad. This instantly famous propaganda image I saw on TV in Brisbane, but now, in this longer perspective, it's clear an American tank is doing the actual toppling, and a ring of American soldiers, their machine-guns facing outwards, keeps the people of Baghdad away from the photo shoot. In its iconic media staging, this simulation is a distant, dishonest relative of the kabuki theatre: both concerned with themes of violence and honour.

Late into the night, we pack needful things into two small, light bags for the journey west across Japan in the morning.

Sunday, April 20

At Shibuya Station, Jo and I are to meet Jen Hill, who will be wearing a red Hawai'ian shirt. The two of us arrive a few minutes early, and I enter what appears to be an unoccupied washroom. But near the door, next to the sink, is a brand-new silvery laptop. I look around and finally spot the owner of the computer standing in front of a urinal twenty-five feet away, his back turned. The Japanese are stunningly unconcerned about theft.

A swollen river of people churns past while Jo and I press ourselves against a station wall. Both of us are beginning to doubt we're in the right place. Then Jen arrives—looking a lot like her mother, Judy—in the chin and mouth—with hints of her father, Murray. Quick hugs and laughter. Jen's medium-length hair is not her mother's bright red, but closer to her father's black. She has the bubbly, obvious kind-heartedness of her mom mixed with Murray's cynical sense of humour. The three of us board the Shinkansen for Nagoya, where Jen has just quit her job as an engineer at Japan Steel.

As we sit down, there's a contretemps at the front of the train. An older Japanese man is shouting at the train conductor, who keeps bowing and apologizing and bowing. Jen says this behaviour is highly unusual, and translates for us. It seems four youthful foreigners—

not understanding the "b" seat designation—sat in the elderly man's reserved seat, and when they moved across the aisle, did not apologize for their error. The train actually leaves the station two minutes late as a consequence of this disruption, an exceptional delay in Japan according to Jen. The harried conductor comes by, bowing to us before taking our tickets, and whatever I want to say to him I can't articulate even to myself. At Nagoya, where we transfer to the train for Takayama, a small boy of about eight comes on and sits down beside Jen. He's riding by himself to the very end of the line, and Jen talks to him quietly, reassuringly, in Japanese. The food trolley passes by with some ice cream that's so cold it'll take me an hour to chip off the serving with the small plastic spoon. Jen explains that "*moippai*" means "another, one more," but "*moipai*" (with only one "p" and unstressed) means the opposite, "I'm full." Jo keeps calling Jen "Judy," the name of her long-ago childhood friend from Kelowna, B.C., mixing up daughter and mother. We can't even handle English here.

It is a cold, clear late afternoon when we arrive at Takayama station. At this altitude, spring blossoms are still out. We taste some sweet dried strawberries sold from an open stall, then cross a vermilion bridge over the lively little river that winds through town. The three of us walk down the main street to our traditional Japanese inn, or *ryokan*, where we take off our shoes and put on tan slippers that pinch my toes and leave my heels hanging over the back. It's not easy to negotiate the narrow stairs in these slippy slippers. Our room is large, with many tatami mats and a TV set. The shared sleeping space is only a sliding door away. I shuffle down the hall to the bathroom where I change into slippers printed with cartoon figures sitting on a toilet. The pale blue urinal is stamped "Toto"—not in Kansas anymore? A little fancier and somewhat updated, the ryokan is essentially as my father described the traditional Japanese dwelling sixty-five years ago in *The Hamilton Spectator*. Written on the eve of World War II, much of my father's cultural description is now overly-familiar, but back then would have been news for most Canadian readers. And, remarkably, my father invites an empathetic understanding of the Japanese, the about-to-be enemy.

Leaving our ryokan, Jen, Jo, and I set out to explore this picturesque mountain town. Turning left down a narrow street that is hemmed in by ancient buildings, we find ourselves in San-machi Suji, the traditional home of Takayama merchants and saké brewers. We stop in at a place where two vats of miso are fermenting, aged one and three years. The free samples are ambrosial, and the women working there become very friendly when I answer their question of where I'm from with "Canada." Three times I go back—the miso is so delicious I can't believe I've (n) **ever** tasted it before. Finally, we exit with many thanks and sayonaras, and enter a nearby shop which has a big brown ball of conifer twigs hanging outside its doorway, the emblem for saké—perhaps because it is heated and reduced by fire? In back of the store there are huge barrels of the stuff whose pleasing roundness might portend the bodily shape of the imbiber. Further along the street, Jen points out two slightly warped, exceedingly tall wooden doors. Behind them, partly visible through a vertical strip of air, is a massive float. Gold and red, this ornate creation is splendidly carved and brocaded—and brought out only twice a year, at the spring and autumn festivals. We won't be here on either occasion, so I can only squint past the high locked doors at an elongated fragment of Takayama's communal life. This fractional glimpse mirrors the limits of this journey, in which I can only guess at the completeness I'm missing.

It's chilly as we walk back to the ryokan for dinner, a cold hard-skinned crispy-smoked fish in a zig-zag shape—that must have been grilled on a stick, accompanied by delicious beef steaks, salad, and, best of all, miso soup. Jen, grinning wickedly, holds up an eye-ball and pops it into her mouth.

Later, after changing into our *yukatas*—beautifully patterned cotton robes of white and navy-blue, with a sash and a dark blue jacket—we, one at a time, walk to the bath with towelettes on our heads. On a low plastic stool big enough for one buttock, I soap and rinse, then step into the bath kept warm by a floating silvery sheet, with a ball of herbs underneath. In my short slippers, I return to pull down the cosy covers.

When working at Japan Steel, Jen lived in a big female dorm, but I'm still worried I'll keep her awake. Jo says I don't snore when sleeping near people I don't know that well. Which category does Jen fit into, this little girl I once knew who has become a woman friend?

"The Japanese Home" by John Harrison

The Hamilton Spectator, September, 1939

Simple Austerity of Rooms Does Not

Clash With an Intense Love of Beauty

This is a picture of the homes and domestic life of the Japanese people in the smaller cities, towns and villages—not those of the dwellers in the larger centres like Tokyo and Osaka. For in the latter places western methods of living and western dress have been adopted to a very great extent; even if it is no uncommon occurrence for a big city business man to change from his suit in the evening into the loose and comfortable kimono of his fathers. We write of the "average" Japanese.

* * * * * * * *

Family life, traditions and customs are markedly influenced by religions of the past and of the present—Confucianism, Shinto and Buddhism. Life in Japan is not individual, but stems from groups of which the family is the smallest unit. This fact is borne out by the remarkable recovery from the devastating earthquake of 1923, a recovery which was expedited by the family system. Persons who suffered in this calamity were able to take refuge with a wide circle of friends and relatives living outside the stricken area.

Their homes are different from ours for two main reasons. First, they are different because of regional difficulties; that is, they must be able to withstand the shock of earthquakes, and let it be said that the Japanese house surpasses all others in this respect except those built with reinforced concrete. Second, they are different because they are adapted to a people whose scale of living, while suited to their needs, does not compare with the level in western countries.

Lath and plaster are the usual materials of a house. Wooden beams are employed to support this structure and the roof. The oriental tendency to do things differently from westerners is to be evidenced even in building. Instead of raising the main portion of the house and then placing the roof on top, the Japanese construct the latter part on the ground and then hoist it into position. When this takes place the owner or the contractor climbs to the roof-top and to celebrate the occasion throws down from here coins and rice cakes to the assembled crowd of children.

* * * * * * * *

One-storey, four roomed homes are the general rule. The outside walls are made of lath and plaster, the inside being divided by sliding panels (fushima), six feet by three, which consists of paper stretched on wooden frames. These can be taken out to make your room larger or smaller. As the Japanese rely on clothing for warmth, only portable charcoal boxes are used for heating. Six feet by three is the standard measure in the house, for this is the size not only for the panels, but of the wooden shutters which enclose the veranda found in most homes and also of the mats which cover the floor. The shutters are closed at night to take the place of the shoji or panels of translucent paper used in the day time in parts where light is needed.

A visitor would almost be frightened by the simple austerity of the rooms. They are devoid of furniture. The floor is covered with mats made of rice straw, which are about two inches thick and which are surfaced with a fine piece of matting. The mats and the covering are bound together by cloth. These are wedged closely together over the loose boards and the size of the room varies according to their number. Bedrooms are unknown. Quilts, filled with cotton wool, are placed on the matting, one or more on the floor and as many as you like on top of you. This makes a comfortable but occasionally draughty bed.

* * * * * * * *

Although the cooking is done on a little charcoal-burning fire box, every house has its kitchen and there the meals are prepared. The rice, when cooked, is put in a large bowl, which is brought to the meal, but with this exception the food is served in individual dishes. The family, seated on the matting (tatami) or on flat square cushions, partake of the repast, which is set on a small table. The use of chopsticks makes the meal a silent one. Fish and potatoes, especially sweet potatoes, and vegetables are the main items of the diet, while bread is still considered a luxury. A favorite dish for foreigners is O sushi, which consists of rice balls filled with chopped-up vegetables and eaten with sauce made from the soya bean, a substitute for vinegar. Green tea is the chief beverage. Served in small bowls, it is delightfully refreshing. Saki or rice beer is drunk during the festival season.

The house is kept clean by the removal of the wooden geta or clogs before entering. These are left in the genkan or porch. On stepping up to the wooden passage leading to the rooms you put on zori or straw sandals, which are discarded when you enter the rooms, leaving only the tabi or ankle high cotton socks, used in place of stockings or socks.

* * * * * * * *

The Japanese are a cleanly people. A great number of the simpler homes contain baths. These are of an oval shape about six feet in perimeter and at least four feet deep. The water is heated by means of a fire in an iron grating at one end. Soaping is done before entering the bath, and as a result one lot of water is sufficient for the whole family. Since nobody uses soap in the bath, and as a constant trickle of cold water comes in, the water is kept fairly clean. The household, from father to servants, bathe in what is practically the same water. The temperature of the water runs from 112 to 120 degrees F. Failing this means of making a toilet, members of either sex can go to the public baths, where, for a few sen, they may wash in a segregated pool of steaming water.

The Japanese house may seem flimsy to us, but it is in fact elegant and graceful. It forms a background for a family life which is conditioned by an atmosphere of dignity and self-control, but which is shot through with a genuine and intense love of beauty.

Monday, April 21

The three of us set off in soft, intermittent rain for the early morning market that stretches along the Miyagawa River, with pink and white blossoms everywhere. A very small, hunched old woman, half-asleep under a clear plastic shelter, stirs when we pause. From this vendor, who's wrapped herself up in a long silk scarf, Jo buys seven tiny bags of seven spices, *shichi mi*. Jen, through a conversation in Japanese, identifies the ingredients: *togarashi* (paprika), white sesame, black sesame, *yuzu* (citrus), *asa no mi* (seed), *sansho* (lime leaf) and *nori*, the seaweed I know from sushi rolls. Jo intends to bring home these spicey sachets as gifts.

This mountain town might resemble Akita, where Ernest's missionary work ended, near the northern end of Honshu. If Japan's main island has the shape of a flexed arm extending eastward, Takayama is at the bicep, Tokyo by its elbow, and Akita near the wrist. Ethel, a long way from Australian heat, reported that on their arrival in Akita the water froze overnight in the kettle which stood on the stove. *Ni ikitai desu Akita*—I want to go to Akita.

We walk on to a little corner shop by another wooden bridge, where Jo examines some antique kimono fabrics. The prices are ludicrously beyond our budget, but the talk in English with the saleswoman

115

continues for awhile. As we're about to go out the door, she calls out to Jo and gives her two small fragments of cloth—because they are "dirty." Maybe the faintest of stains on one, but, to my eye, the other, squarish piece—a former pocket—looks flawless. Likely both from the same kimono material. Against an ochre background, whites, oranges and lime-greens create abstract flowers, perhaps wisteria. A gift of loveliness to a stranger.

We return to our inn for breakfast—another zed-shaped, agonized fish, plus some sharp-tasting mini-fish in a kind of salad. Under Jen's instructions, I crack a raw egg in a bowl, mix in soya sauce, and pour this concoction over some rice. We also eat soba noodles, mushrooms, miso soup, and a roasted onion set elegantly on a magnolia leaf.

I'm reminded of Ethel's wary reaction to Japanese food:

"It is very interesting here to go down to the beach and see the people raking up masses of green seaweed from the water's edge. This is dried in the sun and eaten with rice as a savoury. Some of the Japanese dishes are very nice, but most of it is very indigestible and a good many missionaries have become seriously out of health by taking too much of it.

"Octopus is one of their favorite dishes, but its powers of resistance are great. It would require even a Gladstone one whole day to masticate a mouthful!"

I don't understand her allusion to Gladstone's choppers. Is this a politico-dental reference to the ex-British Prime Minister as a great or untiring orator? History, an infinite regress that can never be traversed.

After breakfast, Jen wants to lead us to a small museum: Takayama Jinya. Originally built in 1615 and used by the Kanamori clan to collect taxes in the form of rice, it has a big granary space. Evenly spaced golden-red beams hold up the ceilings, and confer on the rooms an unoppressive symmetry. The quiet lustre of the hand-hewn wood is as beautiful as the sheen of the porcelain pottery that's set carefully out on the floor. Also exhibited, behind thick ropes, are wooden commodes. This is a culture that even as it innovates tirelessly values all aspects of its past. Jen met the female engineer who saved Japan gadzillions of gallons of water every second by designing an audio tape that automatically plays the sound of rushing water when a woman sits down on the toilet—thus masking bodily noises, so people no longer flush twice.

Jen's keen to visit a "town" of very old wooden buildings, mostly farm houses, that have been transported from different sites in Japan and relocated on a nearby hillside. On this cool morning, while waiting for the bus, we eat *gohei mochi*, sweet sauce on gooey rice, or what Jen calls a "hot" Popsicle. The ten-minute bus ride takes us up to an even chillier mountain setting, and to an odd assemblage of unpainted wood structures which the brochure calls a "reservation." The opposite of Tokyo, this preservation? The ancient roofs are topped with the green of growing grasses. Although the houses have earthen floors and are unpeopled, everyone removes

117

their shoes before entering. For generations, these were the homes of farming families, so visitors do not diss their ghosts.

Yet this outdoor folk museum around a man-made lake is without context, treating as unimportant the original settings. It's the exact opposite of Ninstints in the Queen Charlotte Islands, a UNESCO World Heritage site, where the silver-grey, collapsing buildings and weathered cedar poles of the Haida village devastated by smallpox are left *in situ* to rot. Edged by the wilderness and the sea, the village is mindfully unpreserved as a living graveyard. A sharp, reverberant thwock startles me out of my thoughts. The sound comes from a bamboo contrivance that's like a miniature teeter-totter. Jen says it's a *shishi-odoshi*, a deer-scarer. A tilting bamboo tube fills with water, and is pushed further and further down until, finally, it spills out its watery weight—flipping this end up and clacking the other one down against a rock. No animals visible here. This clever device might be useful back on Hornby Island where Bambi keeps munching our flowering plants. Thwock.

For dinner we go out to a restaurant that has a charcoal grill set into the table. Jo and Jen have saké, while I drink the dark local beer, *biru*. Slowly cooking in front of us is Hida beef, named after the region that surrounds Takayama, and also grilling are chicken, pork, and squid—though these high, interior mountains are about as far away from the sea as you can get in Japan. Amidst all the talk and jokes, I keep seeing Jen as the near perfect sharedness of two divorced parents. Her intelligence is unsurprising, given that her father once taught physics at Caltech and her mother, a math gold medallist at UBC, worked on the Mariner space project, but the wonderful fusion of mischief and considerateness belongs to Jen alone. She has decided to return to the States to study dentistry, perhaps with a focus on children, joining a wish to help people with her skills in technology.

For Jo and I, the great fun of being in the Japanese Alps can't be separated from our good fortune of having Jen as a companion. Are all travel truths then contingent ones?

"News from Japan" by Mrs. Harrison

Australian Board of Missions Review, September 15, 1931

"The climate here [Akita] is quite different from Chiba. We left Chiba in early spring, and arrived here in a blizzard, having gone back to the depths of winter. It took some time to get used to it, as the winds are so severe. They come straight across from Siberia; but now we are past that and into the spring, at least a month later than Tokyo. Very beautiful it is too. Nature seemingly makes up for the long and severe winter. The blossoms are wonderful, wild azaleas everywhere on the hills, and the most vivid green shooting up all around. Akita is very beautiful. A winding river that plays a game of 'follow my leader' all through the town. A lovely park on a hill, the site of an ancient castle; and on the very highest part a wonderful avenue of cherry trees."

Tuesday, April 22

For this last ryokan breakfast, more protein than I'd have guessed possible: salmon, bacon, eggs, and, in the salad, slices of sausage. Later, feeling strangely unbloated, I cross the street with Jo and Jen to visit the Takayama Betsuin Temple, walking under its imposing torii. Yet inside the temple I feel less of an outsider than I do in Christian churches. In Asia, people don't exactly check their secular selves at the door, and this spiritual domain feels unjealous. With the temple seal, I stamp in black ink the book I'm carrying, Nigel Krauth's *Freedom Highway*. Jen tells me I've imprinted it upside down. But isn't that appropriate for an Aussie novel?

Back out on the sidewalk, the three of us pause to pet a golden retriever wearing a zippered, electric-blue disco pant suit. We continue on to the San-machi Suji district, where Jen buys a small Ichii Ittobori sculpture that's carved from yew, a tight-grained yellow wood, polished to a warm glow. This whimsical knicknacky figure combines (according to the brochure) "rustic simplicity and fine workmanship." But this object expresses a Japaneseness I can't relate to. We continue on to the Folk Craft Museum, Fujii Bijutsu Mingei-kan, which has art from China and Korea, as well as that of Japan, and here, at last, my Western eyes can see these three linked Asian cultures as distinct.

In cold rain, we return to the ryokan, and Jen, on behalf of Jo and me, calls a traditional inn in Kyoto—speaking in Japanese to the woman on the other end, reassuring her that we've been "trained." There'll be no breakfast for us in our next lodgings, but we've been accepted. Jen reports that she, for simplicity sake, had to tell the old woman on the other end of the line that Jo and I are her parents. We love the idea of adopting her. Jen would be an ideal daughter: funny, full of moxie, kind, upbeat, smart, and already grown-up.

With our alleged daughter, we hurry to catch the 11:20 a.m. train. Following the twisting descent of the rushing mountain river, the train snakes us back down to the coast, arriving as scheduled at Nagoya at 13:38. Since Jen is getting off here, we hug our good-byes and promise to meet soon in North America.

Jo and I, our bodies and minds in motion once more, head further west on the bullet train, towards the quintessence of Japan: Kyoto. Arriving at its station, the two of us get into a rare spat. Is it travel fatigue or irritation at having to guide ourselves, after laid-back days of irresponsibility? Whatever the cause, we stupidly argue over *which* information office to go to: the small one, right here, or a bigger one, further away, that someone recommended. Maybe unconsciously the two of us are wise enough to wrangle over things that don't matter. After some back-tracking, we talk to a gentle-voiced guy who in near-flawless English locates the Iwanami Ryokan for us on a map of Kyoto, and directs us to the #206 bus. In a reversal of Canadian custom, we enter near the back of this bus and are expected to exit at the front—a cognitive parallel to reading directions? But we're not sure when to get off. Jo hears a scratchy announcement in Japanese for "Gion," the district we're aiming for, so we hurriedly disembark, and find ourselves on a quiet street beside a canal.

We figure out our inn must be on the opposite side of this waterway. We turn the corner, then walk the entire length of a narrow street, Shinmonzen-dori, which is bordered with stores selling art antiques. Then Jo and I come back along its full length once more, searching. I speak to a few un-Englished people, and go into some stores looking for guidance: it turns out we've walked past the Iwanami Ryokan twice. We tilt our heads and gaze down a private stone path that looks untrodden this century. No kanji on the outside of the deeply set-back building, but we venture onto the series of flat stones. At the far end, a tiny, ancient woman who never straightens up holds out some slippers.

I pad down the long hall, but forget to take my slippers off before entering our room. When I ask her where the bathroom is, she scowls at my ignorance, moves sideways to a corner, and with some force slides open a portion of the wall. I feel like an obtuse failure—a Westerner looking for door knobs. The crone leaves abruptly, apparently miffed, shutting us in our room. But soon she comes back, with tea and cookies that she sets out on a low table. Jo and I sip and munch, gazing out at the weeping cherry blossoms that cascade over the canal's flowing light. This might be the best location in Kyoto.

We walk to the nearby gardens of Murayana Park, look in at the shrine of Yasaka-jinja, then visit the Chion-in Temple of Jodo Buddhism. The vast scale of these grounds designed for multitudes I can only experience as diminishment. I prefer the intimacy of the Zen Buddhist monasteries built into the rocky hills of Kamakura, their apparently aimless paths winding up out of view, creating a sense of anticipation and unknowing, like that of travel. When we return down the stone path leading to the Iwanami Ryokan, our inn-keeper is waiting, with two oranges.

This first evening in Kyoto we decide to eat close by. As Jo and I are about to leave, our stooped hostess hustles out and places a stool beside me on the porch—along with two wooden blocks to be used as footrests, and a long shoehorn. I'm a bit embarrassed as she helps me change into my not-so-clean running shoes. For dinner at the Sen-mon-ten, we eat Chinese dumplings, drink Chinese beer, and watch Japanese baseball: the Yoshimuira Giants rallying against the Yakult Swallows. After, we stroll along the broad Shijo-dori, checking out a store that sells nothing but fans, then walk down a well-lit street of red paper lanterns, Hanama-koji, before heading home to Shinmonzen Street and our hidden-away ryokan.

It's dark when we arrive at the porch, the *genkan*, but once more we're greeted by our bent-over hostess. Does she see us coming or wait with infinite patience? Jo and I have a bath, *furo*. The tub's filled to the top, so when I get in, the water overflows, pouring down through the wooden grate in the floor. *O-furo*.

Later, wrapped in our bedding, I hear in the corridor deliberate footsteps. The sound of the aged woman coming closer, closer, then turning away, going around a hall corner to bathe in our common water.

Wednesday, April 23

We wake to the non-urban sound of a duck quacking underneath us—swimming below our waterway porch. Jo and I go to a bakery a few blocks away, buy a couple of sandwiches which we have for breakfast in Maruyama Park, then catch a No. 5 bus heading north-east. We get off near the Ginkakuji Temple, the famed Silver Pavilion. Two-storeyed, tallish, erected on a fairly small footprint, it has swooping wooden roofs on both levels. Graceful architecture that counterpoints two frequently warring cultures, it is dedicated to Kannonbosatu, the Goddess of Mercy. The first floor is built in traditional Japanese form whereas the upper one's in Chinese temple style. Facing east, on the very top of this structure, is a golden bronze phoenix. In the garden below, the sculpted white sand evokes the waves of the ocean, and Mt. Fuji.

The parking lot is filling up with tour buses, so we depart, setting out on the Path of Philosophy located between the foot of the Zen-templed mountains and the city itself. This walkway, which follows Kyoto's narrow eastern canal, offers a liminal space in which to consider below pink and white blossoms the notions of retreat and engagement. Jo and I pause at the serene Honen-in Temple, which has a more meditative feel than the too-thronged Ginkakuji, but we walk on, eager to pursue the Path of Philosophy with its small wooden bridges and subtle curves. Schoolboys in white naval collars and fancy running shoes carry rapier-like instruments to spear any litter. Their shy-smiling English is only slightly less sketchy than our Japanese. When Jo and I near the southern end of the path, I essay a philosophical insight: "We are prisoners of our inn-keeper's devotion." It's weirdly constraining to have someone always there, welcoming you. Ingrate tourist, who—as the French etymology has it—is only going around in circles anyway.

The two of us step off the Path of Philosophy and onto the immaculate grounds of a temple named only in kanji. Twin boar statues flank the building's main entrance. A quick look-see and we're back on the path where we encounter several fox-faced dogs and their well-dressed owners. Akita, the name of this breed of dogs, is, by coincidence, a reminder of the town where Ernest died. We conclude our long stroll at the Nanzenji Temple, where we look up at spectators who gaze down at us, unphilosophically, from the second floor of this huge torii-like entrance structure. On the deep, rising grounds beyond, there are more imposing buildings, but, off to one side, is a relatively modest wood structure named Tenjuan, with a double garden of sand, water, stone, and moss. For half an hour, Jo and I sit by ourselves, attentive and calm.

Then the two of us walk many, many blocks in light rain to a lunch spot (that our guidebook recommends): it's closed. Nearby, we come across a place where we order curry, which the waitress pronounces as "carry." Jo and I decide to catch the #206 bus south to Kiyomizumichi. Alongside dozens of children in spotless, buttoned up naval uniforms, we climb a steep hill to an important-looking temple, then go up some stairs to its wide verandah. It might give a splendid view of Kyoto, but today the city is lost in clouds, so we begin the long descent, down the flank of the hillside on a bendy, falling-away street. On this artistic curve of understated commerce—small wooden restaurants and shops selling traditional ceramics—I'm again moved by the fluid beauty of the street signage.

After a weary bus ride, we at last get back to the ryokan, hoping for tea. But our inn-keeper who's made up our bed has disappeared—so much for my philosophical insight about her fettering devotion. While Jo reads, I watch people with umbrellas moving quickly past, fat raindrops falling into the fast-moving canal. The branch tips of the small-blossomed ornamental cherry do not quite touch the half-dark, rippling surface. Petals drift past.

Lacking energy or imagination, we eat supper at the same gyozo place. This semi-involuntary repetition goes against the reason for travel, the quest for the untasted, but on this evening it is a useful survival tactic. After the necessary meal, we walk west in cold rain, cross the bridge over the wide Kama-gawa River that bisects Kyoto, and encounter the city's neon glare, highlighted by an enormous lit-up plastic sumo wrestler hanging several storeys up from a modern building. He holds a rectangular sign with the figure "100," but we've no clue what this number will buy. The morning's quiet garden monasteries set into the high eastern hills feel very remote from this night district of expensively-dressed shoppers. But for an inhabitant, Kyoto may feel less like a contradiction than an internal dialogue. Perhaps the city is designed to stimulate baffled reflection like the riddling paradox of a zen koan (one hand clapping?), which might lead to enlightenment.

Our inn-keeper waits for us. Reaching an arm as high as she can, the stooped woman wipes off Jo's rain-gear with a towel. Probably like other Western travellers, I can't always fend off the self-flattery of Gulliver, condescending among the Lilliputians. At one of the shrines today I felt I almost had to bend my knees to avoid missing the urinal, and spraying the wall above. And this morning I experienced a twinge of back pain after shaving in a mirror that reached only up to my collar-bone. Now, to assist our ryokan hostess, I bend over double—and she breaks out laughing! All the past small awkwardnesses on this porch vanish in our shared amusement. Her English suddenly improves, and she informs us that Jen has called—she will meet us in two days at Himeji, at 4 p.m., in front of the castle known as the White Egret.

Thursday, April 24

Jo and I wake to more rain, buy a sandwich from the bakery around the block, and head to Kyoto's northern hills. After boarding the crowded #206 bus, I'm standing near the back when a stocky man shoves past, roughly jostling me. The first real rudeness I've experienced in Japan. I figure it must be someone in an early morning grouch on their way to hateful work who doesn't have time for niceties…then realize I've forgotten to create space for others by moving to the *front*.

On a bit of a whim, we choose to go to Tenryu-ji, the temple furthest away. Transferring to another bus that we guess is going in a northwest direction, Jo and I reach the broad Hozu River, which spills down out of the mountains and surges under a long bridge with multiple wooden trestles, which resonates with my idea of Japanese design and geography. I try to articulate this notion as we eat our breakfast sandwiches, but Jo doesn't understand what I'm trying to say, and the river with its mini-explosions of white rapids begins to look a sullen grey-green. In analogy to the way spoken sounds are ignored as meaningless noise if they don't fit within a particular language code, I wonder what I disregard because it falls outside of my category of Japaneseness. At a sudden shower, we move under a conifer loaded with cones that has been wind-twisted into a giant bonsai. I doubt that my neurons would have sparked this association in Newfoundland. As a traveller, I don't like this cooker-cutter pre-shaping of the unencountered; on the other hand, I came here for just such moments of recognition, and felt affinity.

In the on-again, off-again rain, Jo and I enter the nearly empty paths of Tenryu-ji. The high hills hold out this temple and its garden grounds like an offering in a cupped hand. In the drizzle, we walk fairly quickly around these paths, then go into a bamboo forest whose green trunks are more than ten times my height. My gardening experience with bamboo that clumps doesn't prepare me for these substantial trees of glistening green. Increments of white rings notch ever upwards until the faraway tops bend high over our heads, making an airy hallway. Marking off our path, the open curving fence has horizontal, dried-brown bamboo poles that form two parallel lines. Near the base of the giant living "trees," wrapped in dark brown triangles, are dozens of new plants. Small rocket shapes about to take off.

We emerge from this unreal forest, and, as we cross over railway tracks identified in English as the "Romantic Train Sagano Line," I take Jo's hand. High-toned houses appear, then ponds and open fields, and we arrive at the Imperial Palace of Saga Daikakuji. Inside, on gold-leafed screens, are realistic paintings of nature—the opposite of the magnificent bamboo archway in which living trees have become architecture. On a shiny pink-red counter, an ikebana display continues this interplay of the natural and the artful, reminding me of the lovely, bold arrangements of flowers my mother used to create from her large

Vancouver garden. My novel in letters set in the aftermath of the French revolution, *Eyemouth*, pays homage to her, her Scottish heritage, and to the fishing village which her grandfather, James Crombie, sailed from on the *Radiant* with the fleet of open boats in 1881 into what became a cyclonic funnel of wind, and in the rocky North Sea drowned with one hundred and twenty-eight other Eyemouth fishermen.

Out of this journey to Japan, will I be able to create a non-fiction book of comparable worth for Dad? That little boy, separated by an ocean from his parents, who grew up into a handsome rugby player—the captain of Ontario's side—who graduated with an M.A. before he was 21, suddenly found himself fatherless, and, like the rest of his generation, in the midst of a Depression; then World War II, followed by the shock of suburban affluence. Larger than his job, Dad sometimes chaffed at his employment—tried to write short stories. He was the best father in the world whom I, as a grown-up, became childishly pissed-off at for several months for wrecking the myth of our happy family. After leaving Mom, Dad lived alone for a period, took our two sons salmon fishing off northern Vancouver Island, and for a memorable week-long trail ride in the Rocky Mountains.

In the tall vase, the three separated branches of blossoms hold the soft early-spring yellow of forsythia, the slightly bluish-red of azalea, and the tender whiteness of apple or cherry blossoms, half-fallen from a lichen-greened branch. There's a triangulated shape to this floral design that asymmetrically blends earth, heaven, and human. Only at my mother's funeral did tears for my father fall.

To reach the next temple Jo and I need both a bus and a train, so as torrents of rain pound down, we splurge and take our first cab in Japan. The deluge lessens slightly as we enter the grounds of the Ryoanji Temple with its celebrated garden of sand and stones—that we can't actually find! Taking partial cover under a high torii from yet another downpour, Jo studies the temple map, as I (through rain-smeared glasses) note how her wet apple-green jacket matches exactly the spring leaves on a nearby maple. Three or four boys in navy-blue uniforms with brass buttons and sailor collars approach us—quietly ask if we will sign the forms that they carry, attesting to the fact they've spoken with "foreigners." After our chilled fingers have made our signatures, one boy with buck-teeth shyly and proudly holds his transparent umbrella over Jo's head, and together they all guide us to the famed rock garden.

The site's zen-ness is both familiar and startling. Fifteen irregular rocks protrude from a rectangular bed. Photographs haven't dulled a sharp Keatsean sensation that here beauty and truth converge. Bordered by low earthen walls, this "garden" of isolate, rain-darkened rocks isn't made of sand but of crushed white stone. No insistent green of growing is visible, aside from tiny patches of moss that belatedly catch the eye. But the leaves of the trees beyond provide enough of that colour, along with a blossoming pink. The precisely raked, parallel, wave-like markings—both linear and circular—wash up against the interrupting presence of the rocks like an incoming tide.

Under very hard rain, we take the ten minute walk to Kinkakuji, the Golden Pavilion. This small, islanded building—exquisite in its proportion and lustre—has in the heavy rain a subdued, tender quality. It is a golden reconstruction, which followed a violent assertion of the Buddhist doctrine of *anatta*, impermanence. A monk burned down this historic temple in an act that mingled spirituality with craziness, and inspired a novel by Yukio Mishima about purity and obsession. For a second, the rain halts, and there is a pale, ghostly, white-gold reflection of the double roofs upended in the surrounding pool.

Two bus rides later, we're back at the Iwanami Ryokan, where our hunched, aged, solicitous blue-coated matron dries us off. In our room, Jo watches the drama of street life while I fall into an apparently dreamless sleep. When I awake, she describes a vision she had sitting on our waterway verandah. From the flat, unadorned modern apartment across the canal, a geisha in a kimono with traditional make-up glided forth into the fading light. Palely glowing in pink silk, this creature of fabled allure (accompanied by a driver holding a parasol) stepped gracefully down the stairs, slipped inside the waiting taxi, and, with theatrical magic, disappeared into Kyoto's evening. I vow never to take another nap in Japan.

When we go out, it's still wet. Jo and I cross a bridge to Kyoto's west side, which has some lively street action, but it's so drizzly we take shelter in the Maruzen bookstore, whose 9ᵗʰ floor has an unexpected range of English texts, including a superb novel I've taught, Joy Kogawa's *Obasan*. Her subtle images tell with exactitude and without self-pity of the internment of Canadians of Japanese descent following Pearl Harbour. Mostly,

I look through translations of Japanese comic books, *manga*. It's far later than the posted closing time of 8 p.m. when Jo and I, hesitantly, go back out into the rain.

We walk north, then cross back east on a different bridge, searching for the Ichi-ban restaurant. On this side of the river, Kyoto is mute and un-neoned. On the broad street of Sanjo-dori, only a single red paper lantern is lit. Drawn by this light, we push open a small wooden door, and go inside gratefully. Is this the Ichi-ban with *yakitori* as its specialty? No matter, we've found a cosy place. Damp but upbeat, we eat skewers of chicken and beef cooked over charcoal, then return in near-blackness to our inn—where we receive another conscientious drying off. A*rigato gozaimasu.* Then an *o-furo*, with its steaming wet heat, which, illogically, takes the dampness out of my body.

Why would a rainy day of visiting temples give contentment to a non-believer? Why would a missionary delight in physical adventure?

"Up a Japanese Volcano" by Rev. E.R. Harrison

Australian Board of Missions Review, February 7, 1920

"We rolled our blankets round us and lay

down on the straw matting for a short sleep. We got up at half-past one and had another little feed, including some very good Boston beans and soup squares which the doctor had brought with him. It was a beautiful starlit night when we started off again, and pretty cold. The first part of the ascent was very steep, and then we got on the loose volcanic ashes, with a pretty steep slope. The last part was very rough and stony, and we arrived at the top in about three hours, and half an hour before the dawn. The crater is 1300 ft. across and 1000 ft. deep, and as we looked down we could see two big places where the fires were glowing, and all the time there was pouring out a huge cloud of steam and smoke. Sometimes the volcano gets pretty active, and sends out showers of stones for miles around, but of course it was quiet enough when we went up. In spite of the blankets which we had taken with us we felt bitterly cold waiting for the dawn, but we were rewarded with a wonderful view when the sun did spring up. The valley which we had started from was covered with mist, and looked like a huge white lake in a ring of mountains, but towards the east it was quite clear, and green plains and rugged mountain ranges lay one behind the other as far as the eye could reach, the long morning shadows making the country stand out exactly like a tremendous relief map. On my way down the mountain we got a very clear view of the lava beds, one of the 'seven wonders of Japan,' where, in 1783, over a thousand people perished in a great eruption. The lava is nearly 200 ft. thick in places, with great rocks piled up here and there in wild confusion, and as one sees the way in which it began to spread over the plain, and got congealed in the process, it gives a very clear idea of volcanic action. We got back to the tea-house about half-past seven, and were quite ready for another 'lunch.' Two hours walk through the forest we came to some hot springs, so we rounded off the trip very nicely with a good hot bath."

Friday, April 25th

On this misty morning, we say good-bye to our diminutive inn-keeper, whose black sweater has a design in pale blue of a tall, nearly leafless plant. Posing beside me for a photo, her steady dark eyes look up at the camera. Then she leans her head in, its weight against my bicep. I'm moved by this unexpected intimacy. Jo hugs our faithful keeper, then I do: sayonara.

The bus takes us back to the Kyoto train station, where we board the Shinkansen, leaving behind this one-time city of Emperors, this place of inner enlightenment. We speed yet further west on the island of Honshu. In an hour, we reach Himeji, whose castle stands in the wet air like a huge mirage. Above the carefully tended gardens, beyond its wide moat, Shirasagi, the White Egret, wavers like an elongated bird about to take flight. Jo and I begin walking across the extremely spacious grounds to the towering castle, taking forever. As in Zeno's paradox, it feels as if we're always only halfway there. A paradox that's true also of our larger circle journey. Months have elapsed and we're still by the shores of the Pacific Ocean that we set out from. Taking forever. In its double meaning, that could be a great title for a book about getting to *satori*, enlightenment.

The rooms of Shirasagi are dark, but not gloomy—maybe because they're big enough to hold hundreds of massed warriors. For the defenders, shooting arrows or firing guns, the thick walls have gaps in the basic geometric forms: circles, rectangles, and triangles. A minute later I flip open the guidebook and read the same observation in the *Lonely Planet*. Irked at having this mini-perception scooped, I look around for something obscure that the guidebook missed. There's a small iron protrusion on the inside of the castle's stone wall, and I wonder aloud about its function. Jo bends down, raises up a wide wooden shutter, and hooks it onto this jutting metal piece. A Japanese tourist who's been watching this manoeuvre exclaims, "Ah so!" and I'm delighted to hear this phrase of recognition uttered in response to a small act of insight by the Westerner I'm married to.

For two hours, we go up and down the steep stairs of the five-storyed castle before Jo and I tire of examining the military architecture. Outside, relaxing on the grass, we get pulled into a conversation with a couple from Western Australia who recommend a visit to Nagasaki, which I'd like to see—in part because that's where shipwrecked Portugese sailors introduced Christianity to Japan. But Nagasaki is another island away, on Kyushu, and already we're way too short of days.

Under the overcast sky, Jo and I walk back down from the castle to the town of Himeji. In the post office, we're startled by the festive brightness of flowers. Their intense oranges and sheer yellows are outrageous in a setting I associate with slushy boots, harsh lighting, and glum concrete. I sit down and begin writing postcards, when—outside the window—it's Jen! In a work of fiction, such a chance encounter would seem like a lazy contrivance. We had arranged to meet in front of the White Egret an hour from now, but here we are with hugs and joking and an intro to Kenji, a work friend from Japan Steel. He is shyly eager, and thin even for a young Japanese male. He and Jen want to take some pictures of the White Egret, so Jo and I go check out the castle's peony garden. It's raining, but the soft pink flowers are lush and soothing.

With Kenji at the wheel, we set off in Jen's car. A GPS navigation device on the dash directs us further west, towards Okayama. Against my will, I keep staring at the electronic lines simulating the journey instead of looking at the actual geography flashing by the window. We halt to pick up some food, which is **a** lot of fun with Jen to explain what we're buying. The Japanese packaging, textures, and colour tones now look normal to me. Back in the small car, crowded with our packs and new supplies, we begin to climb up a tight, nearly traffic-less mountain road that curls into the clouds. Visibility shrinks down to a body-length, and the GPS pointer swings through 360 degrees, around and around, as if to say, "I give up." Jen figures we must be pretty close to the Hattoji Villa, so Kenji reverses, and we go back to a vague fork, creep forward along a foggy road for a few hundred yards, then stop in the pitch-dark. We all get out, stand around, and stare into the night.

A dim building—Jen goes on ahead, and we follow uncertainly. Somehow she finds a key, and we enter a large traditional wooden structure which has four bedrooms partitioned off by big sliding doors and a communal modern kitchen: the Hattoji Villa.

Subsidized by the government, it is one of half a dozen places designed to facilitate informal East-West encounters, so the Japanese aren't allowed to stay here unless accompanied by a gaijin. Tonight, the entire building belongs to the four of us.

Seated around the hearth in the middle of the floor, we eat a chicken stir-fry and drink large cans of Asahi beer. Kenji's English becomes voluble. Jen shows us photos of a recent hiking trip, then half-familiar images from way back of her long-divorced parents— at that time, our just-married friends at university. While Kenji and I do the washing up, Jo takes a bath in the small, circular tub. I walk down the hall to talk with her, but see only a pink, blissed-out face. Taking forever.

Saturday, April 26

Waking early, I slide open the floor-to-ceiling wooden door, and look at the landscape for the first time. Stepping outside into the wind to take a few photographs, I'm immediately greeted by two smooth-skinned, curious dogs: one white, the other golden. Low hedges mark off the surrounding fields, and beyond these are wooden farmhouses with thatched roofs. This region is apparently used as a film location because it resembles old Japan. Did Kurosawa make any of his eastern westerns here? I walk down into a wide gully, and notice three tubular banners of fish attached to a slender pole flying horizontally in the lively breezes. Part of the spring festivities, these koi.

For breakfast, instant Irish oatmeal, with some brown sugar and maple chunks that Jen brought from America. Afterwards, the four of us explore the terrain around the Hattoji Villa, and climb some stone steps leading to an ancient shrine which in its modest stonework is barely visible. Then, following Jen's fearless initiative, we enter what looks like a private garden— go under an elegantly tiled gate with ornate horns, *chigi*, that curve inward from both ends of the ridge-line. Inside is a huge camellia tree with dark-green leaves, which has shed an extraordinary profusion of double rose-form blossoms, making a large circle on the ground that is petalled an intense pinky-red that

141

none of us wish to walk on. It's difficult to take a boring photograph in Japan.

All at once, we realize we have to rush to make a train connection. The four of us drive away in the sunlight as a strong gust catches the koi pennants, and their tailfins fly high up into the late April sky. We speed on towards a nearby village to catch a train on which Jo and I have reserved seats. Late by one minute! Using her cell phone, Jen downloads a schedule, and calculates how to get us to the next station. Kenji is going even faster now, in what's starting to have the excitement of an adventure flick with a deadline structure. Again, I find myself watching not the undulating, three-dimensional world rushing past us, but our mediatized movements on the small GPS screen. Will Kenji get us there in time? At the town of Shiwanagi, the four of us shout hasty sayonaras as Jo and I jump out and grab our packs. The two of us need a second to figure out which side of the tracks we're supposed to be on, then we board the train for a brief ride, before hustling off again to transfer to the JR rail link to the western edge of the island. Jo had asked me where I wanted to go for our last days in Japan. I was conflicted. Chiba? No, I felt it was more necessary to go in the opposite direction. To Hiroshima.

Sombre thoughts intrude. I try to recall the first time I saw someone murdered in a movie. It must have been the shooting of Bambi's mother. An irremediable sadness that everyone in the audience felt when her animated drawing got shot (off-screen?). Not that many years later, my father, a onetime film reviewer, took our family to see Laurence Olivier in *Richard III*. I had nightmares for weeks. Olivier's terrifying presence as a scheming hunchback taking immense glee in killing innocents probably traumatized me into becoming a Shakespeare scholar. The two smothered nephews looked the same age as my brother Doug and I.

When was the first time I killed something? It most likely was a stepped-on ant, but what I remember in vivid detail is a trout when I was a boy at Yellowstone Park. Almost without effort, this event shifted into a fictional story, "Near Big Timber."

Adam picked up his big rod, walked away along the lakeshore path, stepping underneath whippy branches, over roots and damp logs, with the gravelley noise getting stronger, until he saw the water burble white. He immediately cast his Spin-O-King into a far pool and felt the fierce tug of what he believed to be the rapids—until silver flashed above the river. Suddenly, he realized he had never caught a fish before without his father to free its mouth from the triple barbs. He tried to call over the noise of the rapids. But he kept winding the small black handle on the reel—not too fast—and could see the fish come closer. At the shore it jumped away and he jerked the rod back, only now remembering to keep the tip up. Adam smoothly wound the fish near again, lifted it out of the water, and swung its wet silver life over the high grass, and flopped it down by an evergreen tree.

The gills panted as if a knife had slashed

deeply—almost like a severed head! Adam dropped the rod and bent down just when the fish suddenly flipped itself over. It was too close to the water, so he had to pick up the slippery, slimy thing, and throw it further onto land so it couldn't get away (though it was still attached to the line). Adam forgot to dip his hand in the water first as his father had taught him (so the scales wouldn't come off and the fish could live if he had to toss it back for being too small). But this one was very big, at least the length of a ruler, and it lay inert. Adam leaned forward to look at the dead fish, and, all at once, it wrenched over and he jumped back. Embarrassed at being a scaredy cat (a sissy), Adam searched for a club, like the one in the boat, but here there were only soft branches on little trees. He broke part of one off, and began hitting the frantic fish. But the stick was small and pliable and pretty useless and the fish just flopped more often, covering itself in bits of leaves and dirt, its gill gashes opening and closing like crazy, its eyes staring back at him. But at last, it lay really dead.

Adam took a deep breath, and picked it up by its thin, "V"-shaped tail. And the fish twisted free of his fingers! Hollow inside, he grabbed it and whammed it against the trunk of a tree, but the fish (now somehow off the hook) shot out of his hand, ending up in a berry bush, a foot off the ground, like it was trying to swim through the air back to the river.

Trembling, Adam took it in both hands—one of its eyes hanging half-out. He squeezed tight, and stumbled towards the water, nearly tripping over the rod. With all his boyish strength, Adam heaved it into the middle of the fast-running river. It was swept away, towards the lake, floating on its back. Adam felt hot tears run down his cheeks. When he tried to wash his hands in the cold river, he noticed silver scales stuck to his wet sleeve. He walked back to his rod, stuck one of the triple barbs into the long soft cork handle, and wound the line up so tight the fibreglass rod bowed—just like when there had been a big fish on the end.

Adam walked back to where his father was patiently waiting. Dad asked, "Any luck, Tookie?" Adam told him about the fish he had landed, and how he had thrown it back into the river. His father patted his son's crew-cut head, and said there was a good chance such a tough fish would survive.

Hiroshima.

To arrive at this infamous place of destruction and to be among a million people in lively motion is weirdly unreal. As a Westerner, I half-expect hostility, but none is forthcoming. Jo and I get on a tram, then walk through an animated, colourful shopping area towards the Ota-gawa River. We are staying at the Hiroshima Green Hotel, which is sited at Mile Zero of the A-bomb's blast, just across a bridge from the Peace Park. Inside our small hotel room, I'm mildly shocked to find a brochure advertising porn. But who knows—if we're to believe Freud in his correspondence with Einstein about how to prevent war, anything that gratifies the pleasure-seeking id has value in the cosmic wrestling match of Eros vs. Thanatos. And as a creature of the 60's, I can imagine that the sexually contented might be less enthusiastic about hatred and killing.

Jo and I walk out on the bridge over the Otagawa, and make a left turn onto the Peace Memorial Park delta. At this place of apocalyptic history, our most commonplace symbol of joining, the bridge, means precisely the opposite—a sinister gap in our humanity: the bridge's T-shape might have been the target used by the American bomber. There's a low, circular monument that makes no skyward gestures and holds only rubble, mostly broken brick. The guidebook tells us that Hiroshima's cenotaph "contains the names of all the known victims of the bomb (less the Korean victims)," who laboured in this city during World War II as virtual slaves at the great naval base: "more than one in 10 of those killed by the bomb was a Korean." Politics complicates even sorrow.

We go inside the Hiroshima Peace Exhibit—sickened by the photographic evidence of what we do to one another. Centuries ago, fortuitous typhoons saved Japan from invasion and conquest by Kublai Khan, but (only a few months after I was born) those divine winds turned hellish. A purplish flash and a fireball at 7,000 degrees. Skin imprinted and fused with clothes. Hands and limbs bent as if the bones have melted. Faces made monstrous by an inch of scar tissue. One of the survivors drew another whose burnt flesh had peeled off both arms, and hung now only from the fingernails. Why not despair?

To evade the intolerable, a part of my mind begins to critique the writing on the wall. An allusion to Japan's pre-war imperialism is implausibly softened, "Despite some officials' reluctance, three more divisions were sent into Manchuria." The attack on Pearl Harbour is narrated as if no one really intended a massive air bombardment: "surprised the Japanese people." But in this place of nausea and horror, furtive questions don't alter what my body says about the burning and radiation of humans.

Even if it's into a drizzling rain, it's a huge relief to get outside. Jo and I walk the full length of the Peace Memorial Park in silence. We arrive at some clear plexi-glass structures about the size of phone booths. They contain thousands and thousands and thousands of origami cranes. Suddenly, improbably, and with wonderfully sappy symbolism, the sun breaks through, shining on these myriad pieces of colourful paper children have carefully folded into linked life forms.

We cross back over the river, to the standing remnant of a once-domed building, the Gembaku Domu. Very close to Mile Zero, it's a semi-survivor of the atomic bomb. Stripped of the stone-brick cladding by the blast, the round top now appears notional—a curving barbed-wire sketched against the clouds. Staring upward from behind a black iron fence, I'm distracted by groundskeepers. Two men in yellow hardhats, wearing gloves and a plastic bubble over their faces, drag grass cuttings on a turquoise tarpaulin. Worried about lingering radiation? The lawn around this ruined yet still erect structure is immaculately groomed.

We decide to walk on, northward, in the direction of the Hiroshima Carp's Baseball Stadium, with its huge light standards. Noisy school kids mill about the entrance, holding long pieces of stiff paper that look more like all-star ballots than baseball tickets. We go on to the next landmark, the rebuilt Carp Castle, which is painstaking in its restoration and an impressive building, but has no emotional appeal. In contrast, there's a twisted, ugly thing coming sideways out of the ground by a paved parking lot that very nearly makes me weep. A scrappy little gum tree that, impossibly, must have survived the atomic blast, and stubbornly re-grew itself from buried roots. A miraculous act of survival that is doubly pleasing to me because this never-say-die eucalypt connects Australia to Japan.

A bit aimlessly, Jo and I continue walking, pausing to watch some young players who've just finished their tennis games sweep smooth the eleven golden-brown clay courts of this undespairing city. We stop in at a bistro for a late *latté*. Seated in a corner, we're talking about where we might eat, and a young Japanese woman politely interrupts us. She has overheard us and, remarkably, recognizes our accents as Western Canadian. Yuko teaches English locally, but has been to British Columbia, and mentions she had her purse swiped in a Vancouver food mall. She waves off my apology, and volunteers to take our photos with her cell phone—an amusing technology I've never seen before. After checking out her hair in a small mirror, she then slides over beside me, so Jo can take a photo of the two of us. Now one of Yuko and Jo as I direct this talking device at two smiling women. Our new friend (who's busy tonight) recommends eating at the Okonomi-mura.

The restaurant, only a block and a half away, has the façade of a department store. Its elevator lets us out on the second floor, into a boisterous room. Amidst strong frying smells and loud voices, Jo and I, the only gaijins here, sit down on the only two vacant stools at the big U-shaped table. We order the specialty, hiroshima-yaki. Two women to our left volunteer to take our picture, while the cook pours batter on the steaming-hot surface. It's like we've joined a party. Beside the pale round crepe-like creations are piles of shredded cabbage, dried squid bits, bean sprouts, bacon strips, and a small heap of fresh green onions. The cook flips the spittering ingredients over on the grill, then forms some soba noodles into round patties. With two spatulas to loosen and flip, he slips the first crepe form on top of the noodles to make a round, messy sandwich. He breaks an egg, scrambles it a bit, then throws it on top of his now fat creation, adds a dash of soya sauce, sprinkles on the sizzled green onion, and scoops this large sloppy meal onto a plate that he slides onto the grill's wooden edge in front of us. Hiroshima-yaki. Delicious with the beer. But I'm confused about having such a good time in Hiroshima.

Jo and I go out into the evening and look up at the sombrely bright A-dome, its light flickering across the black river. Back at the Mile Zero hotel, I make travel notes, and listen to the voices shouting in the plaza below our third-storey window. We could be anywhere on a Saturday night, with partying and the promise of love-making.

"The Great Earthquake" by Rev. E.R. Harrison

Australian Board of Missions Review, November 12, 1923

"It is now a fortnight since one of the most appalling earthquakes in the world's history destroyed seven-tenths of Tokyo and practically the whole of Yokohama, besides causing great damage and loss of life in the surrounding districts, and one can begin to analyse some of the sensations of that time and realise the general effects of the disaster.

"At the time of the earthquake we were finishing our holidays at Karuizawa, a mountain resort eighty-eight miles from Tokyo. Suddenly, just before mid-day, the house began to rock violently, and the 'quake was so much worse than usual that we rushed outside for safety, and watched the house and trees swaying to-and-fro, and felt the ground moving beneath our feet. On returning to the house we found that lamps and bottles had fallen down, and saucepans thrown off the stove. Whilst we were picking things up, another severe shake occurred.

For the next two hours they were very frequent, and came with lessening frequency and varying severity for whole fortnight.

"At first we thought that Mt. As-ama, the giant volcano which looms up on the right of our house, was preparing for a great eruption, but no smoke came from the top, and we gradually learned that the centre of disturbance was elsewhere. All communication with Tokyo was cut off, but in this land of typhoons, floods, fires and earthquakes that is nothing unusual, and it was more than a day before we began to realise that a terrible disaster had occurred.

"There followed scenes similar to those at the out-break of the war. There was the greatest anxiety, and groups gathered in the streets discussing the brief scraps of news which came through. Gradually messengers came up with letters or personal narrations, and at once they were surrounded by eager enquirers. Two days after the earthquake, a friend and I packed up some food and tried to get through to Tokyo and Chiba, but it was impossible to get on the train, and then word came through that we could do the most good by staying in Karuizawa. We were on the station from about one to three in the middle of the night, and witnessed one of the remarkable phases which marked the beginning of the general excitement. It had been reported in Tokyo that immediately after the earthquake Koreans had been found setting fire to houses and poisoning wells, and racial hatred spread like wildfire.

"Living in safety and comfort on the brink of so much suffering and destruction, we felt particularly helpless and ineffective, and it was a relief to organise day and night shifts to give food and drink to the refugees as they passed through the station. This line, together with a small branch line to the Chiba peninsula, was the only means of exit from Tokyo, and even then in the early stages people had to walk about sixteen miles to reach it. So the trains came up day and night as fast as they could, men, women, and children herded together in passenger cars or open luggage trucks, riding on the roofs, on the buffers, in front of the engine—anywhere they could manage to cling on. When you remember that the aged and sick, as well as those injured by the falling buildings, or by fire, were amongst the crowds, you can imagine how pitiable was the condition of many. It is estimated that in less than ten days over a million people left Tokyo.

"Nine days after the earthquake I got through to Tokyo with the Rev. F. Macrae, an Australian Presbyterian missionary in Korea, who went down to see if he could help the Koreans. It is true that for the latter part of the journey we had to ride in an open luggage truck, but apart from the presence of soldiers with fixed bayonets on the bridges and stations, the outer suburbs of Tokyo only looked as though they had suffered from a severe storm and occasional fires. But as we walked along to a friend's house, a huge wall thrown across the road, and then the wrecked interior of the house itself, gave us some idea of the tremendous forces that had been at work. It was fire, however, more than the earthquake, which had done the most damage and caused the greatest loss of life in Tokyo, and when we got to the top of Kudan Hill the sight was simply appalling. The view from Kudan Hill was one of the sights of Tokyo, and as we had lived in that neighbourhood for a year, it was perfectly familiar to me. Now, instead of the crowded wooden houses, with tall buildings and offices here and there, everything was wrecked or burnt—as far as the eye could reach a veritable valley of desolation. On the Kundan Hill itself, and here and there amongst the ruins, refugees had put up pathetic little shelters with a few boards or a few sheets of corrugated iron, and one family—more fortunate than the rest—were living in an abandoned motor car.

"In the place where the Home Office used to be, we found only a heap of ruins, so we walked along the wide road between the Imperial Palace and the Tokyo Central Station to the Imperial Hotel. The roof of the palace appeared to be badly damaged, and the huge open space in front was crowded with people living in tents and all kinds of temporary shelters. The station looked much the same as usual, but the group of big modern buildings in front of it all showed evident signs of damage by earthquake or fire. The Imperial Hotel, a new building, showed hardly a crack, and had become the centre of all the foreign and a good many Japanese activities. The American Embassy had been burnt out, and the British Embassy rendered more or less uninhabitable, and the headquarters of both were established in the hotel.

"After going with Mr. Macrae to see Viscount Goto (the Minister of Home Affairs), a doctor friend motored me through the devastated area to Kameido, from which I got the train to Chiba. On my return, two days later, I walked for two solid hours, from Kameido right across the city to the Bishop's house, and with the exception of the damaged group of buildings near the Tokyo station, the whole scene was one of utter desolation. In the poorer parts of the city, where the buildings were almost entirely of wood, not a stick was standing, the only things rising above the ashes being charred safes here and there. If you will think how far you can walk in two hours, and then try to imagine a wilderness of burnt-out dwellings on either side as far as the eye can reach, you will get some idea of the dreary scene of desolation. Chiba, itself, by some freak of the earthquake, was comparatively unharmed. The station had nearly collapsed, and a crack four inches wide ran right along one platform, but the city itself did not look nearly such a wreck as it did after the great typhoon of 1917. Yet forty miles to the south of us the big town of Hojo had only three houses left standing and a thousand people were killed. At that place, too, the coast was said to have risen twelve feet in parts, and a large tract of land was suddenly added to the town. Our house must have looked a bit of a wreck at first, for most of the plaster on the walls was cracked or tumbled down, and a good deal of glass was broken; but a couple of men and a woman had been at work for two days cleaning up, and the floors were all clean and tidy when I arrived. The roof had suffered very little, so the place is quite habitable. The plaster in the church was cracked, but very little of it fell down, so we shall be able to carry on all right. But the great thing was that all our people were safe and unhurt, and their houses very little damaged.

"One of our Christians, who was in Tokyo at the time of the earthquake, had had a wonderful escape. The first two stations on the Chiba railway were wrecked, and he tried in vain to make his way along the line. Then he tried to get off the line into a street, but a locked door prevented him, and he made his way back to a large park, spent the night there, and reached home the following night. Had he been able to get through that door he almost certainly would have joined a crowd of people who flocked to an open space near a big military clothing store. These poor people thought that they would be safe there, but fires gradually crept up from all quarters and over thirty thousand perished in that one spot.

"The Japanese authorities deserve unstinted praise for the plucky and efficient manner in which they handled the terrible situation as a whole. Martial law was proclaimed almost immediately, and the help of the soldiers was an untold blessing. When I passed through the city there was perfect law and order, the roadways had been cleared, and the gruesome task of cremating the dead had been almost completed. Profiteering had been most severely dealt with, and there seemed to be a plentiful supply of cheap food. The situation in Yokohama was much worse, but considering the almost total destruction and the paralysing blow which had been struck at the capital, this was hardly to be wondered at.

"It is a matter for deep thankfulness and wonder to be able to report that in our own Church (the Nippon Seikokwai) all the workers, both Japanese and foreign, are safe. Churches and school buildings have, in many cases, been totally destroyed, but losses like these have been met with a cheery optimism, and the desire is greater than ever to bring to the Japanese people in this great crisis the inspiration and comfort of the Christian faith.   E.R. Harrison"

Sunday, April 27

On this sunny Sunday morning we walk around shops that are mostly closed, but I get a little bun at the 100 yen store. At a fancier bakery, where I buy a croissant, I'm startled by a fresh, thick-crusted loaf of French bread that has the word, "Hiroshima," in raised capital letters—highlighted by a band of white flour—on its bomb-like shape.

Jo and I board the tram for the JR train station, where we get off and eat our take-out breakfast by the A-bomb fountain. More accurately, it is two fountains, side by side, under a pair of huge shiny stainless steel mushroom caps. Instead of the water shooting up, it rains down—very hard—from above. That symbolism is clear, but why its twoness? The design's doubleness could signify Hiroshima and Nagasaki—or maybe convey the useful concept of reflection itself. The tall trees bordering the plaza have very green, very healthy foliage. Jo and I, with nearly the full width of Japan to traverse today, climb on the bullet train for the long ride back to Tokyo.

Speeding smoothly east, I read *The Daily Yomiuri* and catch up on play-off scores in basketball and hockey, then check out the literary pages, which feature a review of a comic book about the Western male in Japan, CHARISMA MAN, created by Larry

Rodney: "Back on his home planet of Canada, our hero was just another average guy ... but when he landed on Planet Japan he became ... CHARISMA MAN." The reviewer, Margaret Layman, asserts that, "Everyone knows at least one—the nebbishy gaijin male, who was probably voted least likely to get a prom date in his high school year book, yet who somehow manages to transform himself into a superstud earning princely sums simply by 'teaching' his own language." If a new country, why not a new self? Fantasies of transformation must be secreted away in every traveller's baggage. My grandfather projected outward his inner dreams of metamorphosis, onto an ancient, mostly resistant culture. Are ESL teachers, the new missionaries, more successful?

Writing some postcards, I think about Ernest sending letters to Australia from his third home, Japan. I reflect on my grandfather's extended account of the Tokyo earthquake—estimated to have killed 150,000 people. In the unimaginable heat of Hiroshima, 80,000 were dead in an instant and, over the next several years, about that many again dying painfully from injuries and radiation. No useful perspective on such calamitous horror is possible. But I'm troubled by how even in the midst of a cataclysmic earthquake, Japan's racism towards the helpless Koreans was heightened, and my grandfather's Christian faith was strengthened. We humans are desperate for beliefs.

This interminable train journey across Honshu is making me restless, and we're only as far as Nagoya, Jen's former workplace. Jo and I each order a boxed lunch, *bento*, one of Japan's everyday works of art, and try to figure out an appropriate gift for Pat de Volpi. We can't hit on anything for his uncluttered apartment, so I read some xeroxes. Quickly I realize my liking for this land's beauty—and for these people of deep courtesy—is only a shadow of my grandparents' love for their adopted country. In the *A.B.M. Review* on February 15, 1932, Ethel voices an attachment that is blindly patriotic:

"Our winter has commenced in real earnest. It has snowed every day for a fortnight, and it apparently intends to do the same all through the winter. But merely the snow would be too uninteresting, so the Akita climate gives us a varied succession. We have snow, hail, sunshine, and rain in quick alternation. The carts are already exchanging their wheels for runners, and very soon the rickshaws will be superseded by small conveyances also on runners and pushed from behind.

"We have been very distressed lately about the sufferings of the Japanese soldiers in Manchuria. Five hundred went from Akita—all about twenty-one or twenty-two. The ground is already frozen six feet deep in Manchuria, and we are sending them as many warm things as possible."

In her humanitarian sympathy, she is unconcerned that the invading Japanese army—despite a pledge before the League of Nations—has formed the puppet state of Manchukuo, forcing millions of Chinese into slave labour building railways and bridges. My grandmother would have been unaware of experiments with bacteriological weapons and (alleged) vivisections without anesthesia. From a post-colonial sensibility, it's hard to imagine that only two generations ago imperialist values were a "given," and the goal of world domination, laudable. How naively culpable will we look a lifetime from now?

In a later volume of the *A.B.M. Review* (February 1, 1937), it a shock to see, inside an oval frame, my grandfather's photograph with the circling broad white collar and the wire-frame glasses—the same picture the journal printed twenty-two years earlier—but identified now as the "The late Rev. E. R. Harrison." This man who I've just come to know is gone:

> "It is with deep regret that we announce the death in Japan of the Rev. E. R. Harrison. The details are meagre, but it appears that Mr. Harrison and his wife were on holiday in the hills, and he received injuries whilst skiing on January 19th. We extend our sincerest sympathy to the widow and relatives of the late Mr. Harrison."

But a month after this obituary comes a letter from the dead, and Ernest springs back into life

> "Many thanks for the kind Christmas gift from our friends in Victoria. The money order arrived this morning, a full month after your letter, so at last I can duly acknowledge its receipt. It is very good of you to remember

us year by year. And I can assure you that we don't forget you. I hope you had a very successful summer school at Ballarat. It is rather difficult to picture the hot Australian Summer just now, for after many delays winter has set in with a vengeance, and a snow-covered, thatched house seen from my study window looks like a Christmas card. A bitterly cold wind is blowing, but in almost an hour's time I am off to the hills with a party of friends for ski-ing. During the last month or so we have had more than our usual share of disasters in this part of Japan. Nearby, Aomori, a leper hospital was burnt down, but all the 678 patients were saved. Then a two hundred feet dam burst in the middle of the night at the Osarizana copper mine, and over four hundred people were killed. At Noshino, one of my stations, over 130 houses were burnt, and the fire swept right up to our church buildings, but fortunately was checked in the nick of time."

After the finality of an obit, it is a strange consolation to hear Ernest's voice lifting off the page. Words can outlast lives. It is odd, though, to hear my grandfather speak of a fun holiday of skiing with friends within the context of disasters, fires, floods, and the Biblical misery of lepers. As well, it's ironic that this letter, belatedly, foreshadows his own death.

The bullet train finally makes it to Tokyo Station where Jo and I get off—only to transfer to the subway line. We've decided to go on a lengthy detour to the

Edo-Tokyo Museum to buy its catalogue as a gift for Pat. I'm too wearied to make a late-afternoon dash to Chiba. But at the apartment, cheerful greetings from Pat—and from Fabiola and Carlotta who've just returned from their week-long trip—buoy me up, and when a NHK friend of Pat's drops by, it becomes an impromptu celebration, with present pleasures displacing a concern with the past.

Mark, who was born in Aylmer, Québec, tells me he's inherited Writer's Disease. I treat it as a joke (and a possible self-description) until he explains that Reiter's Syndrome with its arthritic pain is the male equivalent of Crohn's Disease, which tends to affect females. Carlotta colours away in her book and Fabiola orders in some pizzas. Jo and I go down to the neighbourhood store for Sapporo beer and strawberries. Pat says the Japanese don't have this kind of spontaneous get-together. Everything has to be just right? But I remember Jen's comment on their adaptability: they hit a wall and go in another direction. Mark who can be quiet without being shy, and savvy without being cynical, suggests that the Japanese are stoic. After the amazing upbeatness of Hiroshima, I'm most struck by their resiliency, the sheer bounce-back. This low-key last-night party stretches out pleasantly—followed by mad packing past midnight. In the morning, Jo and I have to be on a flight to another continent.

"Resumé from Bishop Binsted's letter to Dr. Wood, Church Missions House, in New York" [January, 1937], in the possession of Noel Harrison

"On Wednesday, January 13th, about 6 P.M. I received a telegram from one of the vestrymen of Church in Akita, saying Mr. Harrison had been hurt while skiing (about three or four miles outside of City). Took the 10 P.M. train to Akita that night, arriving 11:45 A.M. Thursday. Found Mr. Harrison in small hospital, entirely conscious, but paralyzed from chest down. The doctors told me two vertebrae had been dislocated and fractured.

"They brought him to the Hospital on a stretcher, by horsedrawn sled, but it took three hours altogether, and because of this long exposure in the cold, he caught a bad cold which added to his distress. Upon arrival, I found practically the entire Church congregation assembled, hoping to be of service to Mrs. Harrison or the doctors. I have never known greater devotion or experienced more kindness, shown to Mrs. Harrison and myself, not only by the Christians, but the entire community.

"Doctor Nakamura agreed with me that it would be wiser to take him to Tokyo, where we could have more satisfactory x-rays, and better nursing care; if Mr. Harrison lived, nursing would be of the utmost importance.

"Ropes were slung under the iron bedstead, and ten men, putting long poles through the ropes, carried Mr. Harrison in his own bed, from his Hospital room, with no shaking, to the train, where he was put in a mail car the Station Master had procured for us.

"Between the long exposure after the accident, and having to lie perfectly flat, in one position, hypostatic pneumonia, which had doubtless been developing, made itself more and more apparent Monday night, and for a time he was very low. Tuesday morning, he rallied, and seemed much better during the day, but Tuesday evening he grew steadily weaker, and at 11:40 P.M. he quietly passed away. I am sure he realized his condition, because he gave me all necessary instructions about his will, insurance, etc. He spoke frequently of the boys and Betty, and hoped they would be able to finish their education. When he knew he was facing the end, he said, 'Bishop, it's all right; I am not afraid; take care of Ethel'. Mrs. Harrison and I were with him until the end."

Monday, April 28

Pat gives me one of his favorite books, Alan Booth's *The Roads to Sata: A 2000-Mile Walk Through* Japan, and rides the elevator down with us. Our farewell hugs feel warmer, and truer, than those of our greetings— then Jo and I hustle along side streets, late. My back twinges from wheeling too fast the heavy, unbalanced pack strapped to the flimsy carrier with its tiny wheels. But we make pretty good time to Gakugai-Daigaku Station. Alongside Jo, I swing myself and my pack into the car's rush-hour jam. Careful not to miss our stop, we transfer at Shibuya, get off at Shinjuku and board the Narita Express—reversing the direction of two week's ago. This whole trip's about going backwards.

On the ride to the airport, the first stop will be Chiba. "There are few compelling reasons to visit the area," according to *Lonely Planet.* Yet paradoxically, this suburb south-east of Tokyo is the initial setting for maybe the most prescient novel of our time, *Neuromancer,* by William Gibson, who coined the term "cyberspace" and anticipated the internet: "The black clinics of Chiba were the cutting edge, whole bodies of technique supplanted monthly, and still they couldn't repair the damage...."

We slow, then halt at Chiba, the childhood home of my father and uncle. One dead almost twenty years, the other in his late 80's. What was once casually and irrefutably true, "the boys," is now poignantly false. Reading words against time creates dislocation as well as connectedness. I can't step off here now or we'll miss our international flight. But isn't that why you came so far and burnt so much jet fuel? Lens against the glass, I take a photo of the Chiba train station with its round cement pillars and supporting cross-beams, painted in oblique, alternating segments of white and black. On a square red banner, there's a character inside a circle I don't understand. The train waits a few more minutes, but no one gets on or off. Passengers settle into their tilt-seats, read newspapers. Few bother to look out the large windows.

Another train rushes into Chiba station, pointing in the opposite direction—on its way to Tokyo. It halts on the far side of the wire fence separating the two sets of tracks. I wish I, like Ernest, could view life as a pilgrimage to the gates of eternity. Our doors slide shut, and our train accelerates away as I click another photo. Wide apartment blocks in dispiriting grey slide past, screened now from the rail lines by a row of green conifers, then open land of unplanted rice fields lying under surprisingly clear, reflective water. A journey, then, as it should be: both full and incomplete.

Soon, the Shinkansen slows for the international airport stop. Jo and I grab down our packs from the overhead rack and hurry off the train. In the airport lounge we wait to board our 12-hour flight to Europe and I think back to the Zen garden at the Ryoanji Temple. My memories of it inseparable from the heavy rains and the boys in sailor suits who guided us to the wave-like lines of raked gravel that became eddying circles where the wind-and-water-hewn rocks jutted up out of an imaginary sea. Like these islands of Japan that are home to my grandfather's ashes. A garden of stones in the Pacific.

Our flight number is called. When my grandmother left Akita, the women of the village presented her with a lovely kimono they had sewn. Alternating with exquisite floral motifs are sinuous blue wave patterns. And on the obi (the belt) is a very untraditional motif: a ship with red, square-rigged sails.

PRAGUE: THE COLOURS OF A VIOLIN

. . . even though his left hand is missing

Tuesday, April 29, 2003

At the Czech frontier, the young uniformed guard who's just boarded the train looks stern when Jo and I can't produce all the documentation. We scramble through the flat top sections of our packs. We have about given up when Jo comes across the missing papers, and the now smiling border guard stamps our flimsy border cards before stapling them into our passports opposite the shiny "Vizum" for the "Česká Republika," which is glued onto the facing page. Relieved at not having to play the heavy, he then hands us a slip of paper: "IMPORTANT!! Bearers of Czech tourist visas for up to 90 days must register at the Czech Immigration Police within three working days upon arrival...." Despite Vaclav Havel's Velvet Revolution and its official resuscitation of the joyful traditions of Bohemia, the paranoia of the Soviet Union lingers.

At the main train station in Praha (as I'm learning to pronounce this city), a man in uniform points his gun at the swirl of passersby that includes Jo and me. We dodge touts trying to sell us accommodation, buy some subway tickets from a corner store, and ride to the Museum stop. Our small hotel has a huge clean room with two double beds, a bath and two toilets, and, best of all, a view of the Museum—one of many elegant buildings in this rare European city to have escaped World War II bombing. Our overly gracious room, unfortunately, is only available for two nights since May 1 is a big holiday in this country. Another hangover from Sovietization?

Ethel Mercer was here well before Stalin. But when? In corresponding with the Prague Conservatory, I received this answer back in January from Ales Kanka, Deputy Director:

> "Our student register, that is located at our school, starts unfortunately from 1912. According to the Czech archives legislation we had to deposit all the older materials into Prague Municipal Archives. Therefore I can not give you any reply to your question. Your grandmother could have been either Conservatory student, or private pupil of Prof. Sevcik.
>
> Perhaps, you could find some kind of information during your stay in Prague on Spring."

Like every other spring tourist, Jo and I stroll down Wenceslas Square, which turns out to be a tilted, elongated rectangle, bordered by lovely architecture. Cities, I'm reminded, were once thought of as sites of civilization instead of as a sociological cliché for alienation. Yet such an upbeat view of Praha may be naïve since it has had a long history of mass murder.

Near the lower end of the thronged "square" we go into a travel agency, and with difficulty manage to arrange a stay in Praha for two more nights, at a hostel, but it, too, is booked up on May 3, our final night here. We buy tickets for a concert "on the stairs" that's taking place in twenty minutes at the National Museum, and hurry back up to the top of Wenceslas Square—then climb even further to the neo-classical building that's high on the hill beyond. Inside, we find a space on the marble stairs. The chamber ensemble and a piano squeeze into a landing area several steps below, and music begins. But soon I'm mentally drifting off, around the interior architecture, my eyes more engaged than my ears. Sorry, Ethel, but I'm tired and so is the repertoire—Bach's "Air," Vivaldi's "The Four Seasons: Winter," Dvorak's "Humoresque," etc.— and the musicians play without verve. During the last forty hours, our only rest has been a few hours on the plane from Tokyo, and one or two more on the midnight train from Paris to Frankfurt. In an hour and ten minutes, the listless concert's over, and Jo and I walk outside into a cool rain.

We skirt a harsh, blocky Stalinist structure that has dozens of armed guards— identified on the map as "Radio Free Europe (former Federal Assembly)." It looks sliced and pounded together by a sickle and a hammer. A potential military target? The only real clash seems to be one of aesthetics, between this bunker-like eyesore and the nearby Prague State Opera with its Greek columns. On the wide triangular section at the top, the tympanum, a low-relief sculpture has Orpheus riding a winged horse. The music of his lyre nearly rescued Eurydice from the underworld of shades, but, tonight, all those chamber strings—two violins, a viola, a cello, and a double-bass—couldn't bring Ethel back from the dead.

Jo and I decide to return to the travel booths

in the main train station, in quest of a room for our fifth night in Praha. We approach a man with shiny black hair in the cubbyhole at "Easy Travel." In strong, idiomatic English, he says, "I'm thinking and I'm thinking, but I can't think of anything." At last, with a shrug, he mentions a place whose price is far below the modest figure Jo stipulated, so we pay for it on the spot. How bad can it be?

In the dark we sidestep a few loud drunks, and walk back to the Pension Museum Bed and Breakfast. Ethel, I reckon, came by steamer from Australia, then by train (as we did) to this land-locked country. An adolescent girl, by herself, except for a violin?

Interview with Noel Harrison at Delta, BC, November, 2002:

N: I'll give you a little background information on her. Her father was a civil engineer. What his particular work in Australia was I do not know. She, Ethel Hannah, was one of five children, she being the third child. Her particular skill was in playing the violin, which she taught professionally. During the course of her learning she had spent one year in Prague. In those days of course you took a vessel to Prague and took about five weeks to get there and took about five weeks to get home. She studied with a world famous teacher called Chevjik.

K: By family mythology, I thought it had

been Efrem Zimbalist, Sr.?

N: No connection, no.

K: How do you spell that?

N: I'll try. Say, C-H-E-V-J-I-K, phonetically, you know. I'll give you one small aside on him which may be of interest to you. When I started working for the Alaska Pine Company in 1940 there was this family from Czechoslovakia, that had been in the timber business in Europe, the Koerners, K-O-E-R-N-E-R, and I worked with a nephew of theirs who happened also to play the violin and one day I mentioned to him about my mother and her violin-playing and referred to the fact that she had spent this year in Prague, and Bernie had played there, and he said, well, who was her teacher? And I gave him that name, Chevjik, and he kind of leapt off the floor, just with sheer interest at hearing this name mentioned because to him he was just, you know, the outstanding or one of the finest teachers there was.

Wednesday, April 30

A Mozart of a city. The blocks of harmonious buildings in bold yet subtle colours act almost like musical bars, give measure to the city's on-going melody. Jo and I pause in the vibrant openness of the old town square— just as a mechanical skeleton on the famous clock-tower pulls a cord to ring in the hour. At the two green windows, twelve apostle figurines appear in procession, a reminder of both mortality and salvation.

Across the plaza, a sign points to the birthplace of Franz Kafka. This self-effacing novelist who asked his executor to burn all his writings has become a poster boy for Czech tourism. At a nearby bookstore, I speak to a friendly, long-haired woman working there, who gets genuinely excited at the name of Prof. Chevjik. I ask if she might translate an e-mail letter from the Prague City Archives, and she tells me "*klaverni*" means "piano," and "*zpevu*" is "voice," and that the Konservatore Praha has no record of my grandmother during the period, 1900-1910. These dates, as I now realize from my Australian research, are too late.

Jo and I walk west to the Vltava River, which placidly flows north through much of Praha before bending east. Smetana, a nationalistic composer, took this waterway as the title and subject of his best known piece—though ironically known throughout the world by its German name, "Moldau." The ancient sandstone bridge, *Karlův most*, doesn't permit cars, but the Charles Bridge (as it's translated) is anything but pedestrian with its bronze statues, arches, and intriguing bas-reliefs. Kafka in a letter interprets one of these sculptures as being expressive of the human condition: St. Procopius, with an angry devil harnessed to his plough, tills a rocky field.

High on the ridge beyond the river and to our right are the spired, astonishingly ornate cathedral and castle. On the far side of the bridge, Jo and I eat some take-out lunch in a riverside park as we contemplate climbing in the fictive footprints of K., land surveyor and anti-hero of Kafka's novel, *The Castle*, whose quest for understanding is defeated by the labyrinthine indifference of vague authorities. We watch a boy of about five running around the grass, happily playing tag with an older sister even though his left hand is missing. Like Kafka's land surveyor, I am still trying to figure out the dimensions of this world.

Jo and I visit the park's pay toilet (5 koruna or crowns), then start up the very steep hill towards Prazsky Hrad, the castle which dominates the city. A little exhausted, we make it to the top with its conglomeration of remarkable buildings. For some obscure reason, I touch the hard wall of the tall castle that once had the power to reward and punish, to let in or keep out. From the extensive Royal Garden, we survey the river below, which here begins its large half-loop east. Jo and I enter the Cathedral of St. Vitus, whose 100 metre tower filters the sky's light through stained fragments of glass that re-tell in translucent colours Bible stories I haven't quite forgotten.

From these commanding heights, we make the long descent to the Charles Bridge, and thence with weary feet to Wenceslas Square, where, for not much more than the cost of a movie, we buy some opera tickets. How does the economics of this work? Back at the Pension Museum I nap so solidly I would've slept through the beginning of *La Bohème* if Jo hadn't roused me. Outside in the rain pattering on Wenceslas Square, I buy a tasty sausage and a can of Coke before we hurry on to the building previously known as the New German Theatre, then the Grand Opera of the Fifth of May, later still the Smetana Theatre, before now becoming the Prague State Opera. These name changes, I'd guess, pretty much encapsulate the country's tangled modern history. The interior of the opera house, although a little time-worn, still looks splendid with a giant chandelier, dark red seats, and gilt paint everywhere. The production is also opulent with dozens of singers, a full orchestra, Playboy bunnies, performers being lowered from the heavens, and a giant inflatable silver rhino. There's much vivid fun in this staging of bohemian existence, but I'm grateful my violinist grandmother escaped the harsh poverty of the artist's life dramatized in the opera.

On the way out, we look at some black-and-white photos of Caruso—and Dame Melba. Did Ethel, as a student in Prague, hear her fellow Melburnian perform, or was my grandmother-to-be already back in Australia?

"In 1900, on April 18, the legendary Australian soprano, Nellie Melba (1861-1931) performed as Violetta in *La Traviata* . . . a role supplemented with the mad scene from *Lucia di Lammermoor*."

Maybe Ethel listened from on high in the very seat I'd occupy a century later, and perhaps (like myself) dreamed of a success that never fully arrived.

Thursday, May 1

Jo wakes up and says, "I want to go home." She is not joking.

Although I've shaped much of our itinerary around the retracing of my father's family, the burden of improvising daily the necessary travel arrangements in foreign countries has mainly been hers. Add to this the exhaustion of jet lag, three months of endless walking, and…I don't want to return.

A massage improves her mood a little, but not Jo's outlook. She simply doesn't want to be here anymore. Jo says that she thought that when she got to this age she would be wise. With tightness in my chest and a knotting in my gut—but acting as if these physical symptoms are absent—I go over to the hotel desk to talk to a young guy who speaks some Italian. He books us a place in Venice, four nights from now. Jo says nothing for or against this manoeuvre. Today we have to move somewhere else in Praha or go home. Travel has become travail.

We shoulder our packs and walk silently to the metro. "My God, what an exhausting job I've chosen," exclaims Gregor Samsa, the anti-hero of Kafka's *The Metamorphosis*. "Travelling around day in and day out. It's way more irritating work than the actual work— worrying about the train connections, a bed, the

181

irregular meals." He'd rather turn into a bug. Gregor Samsa's sister played the violin and, more like Orpheus than Eurydice, her music led him out of his room and, temporarily, out of his insect nonexistence.

Jo and I ride to a station with a double-barrelled name before transferring to the tram line, and finally get off at Nuselská Radnice. I lead the way to the Alia Hostel, which is—thank God—fairly bright. Jo doesn't want to head back downtown to the touristy bustle of Wenceslas Square, so we go out for a short walk. Most of the stores are shut and the sidewalks are empty, probably due to the May 1st holiday. We stop in at an internet centre, have a coffee, and try to connect up with home. My Prague research on my grandmother is going nowhere, and I'm starting to feel like Kafka's dung beetle or whatever. Jo and I finish e-mailing and cross a deserted street to a restaurant where we're the only customers.

Back at the Alia Hostel, the woman states in response to my query, "There's nothing to see around here." We go out anyway for a second gentle stroll around the neighbourhood, and discover among the Stalinist concrete a couple of attractive neo-baroque buildings and a pretty little park. Later, on our way to the opera house, Jo's first smile of the day, at a *trompe-l'oeil* tram shelter. It is painted up to look like a real apartment, with flowers in a vase, a bookcase, framed art on the wall, and a comfortable-looking couch upon which three living men sit, not looking at each other. A surreal home for strangers waiting to go somewhere.

Tonight we're watching *Aida*, Verdi's opera about enslavement, and beloveds being buried alive.

The acoustics and sightlines are fine from the centre of the 3rd row of the balcony, but the production is formal and stiff—cadaverous. It could be our mood or maybe a European notion of ancient Egypt as monumental, but there's no breath of lightness. Or perhaps it's a consciousness of what's going on in the Middle East (though Iraq hasn't been in my brain for over a week).

Friday, May 2

At the Alia, this place for "others," there are no real cooking facilities. No pots or pans. Plastic cups and plates are only available from the office "for hygienic reasons." I purchase a microwavable cheese and bacon concoction for breakfast. Jo, wisely, is not hungry.

Again we set out on the tram, a form of transport I associate with Melbourne—and Ethel. We disembark in the Josefov area, just under the bend of the Vltava River, near a huge, neo-Renaissance building, the Rudolfinum. Ethel probably studied inside this grand place of arched windows, Corinthian columns, and a broadly curved façade. It's home now to the Czech Philharmonic Orchestra, but for almost a century this was the site of the Prague Conservatory where, in 1891, Antonin Dvorak joined the faculty to head up the composition department, and later became the school's director. Famous students of this era included Josef Suk, Rudolf Friml, Franz Lehar, Jan Kubelik, and Otakar Chevjik, Ethel's semi-fabled teacher. On the lawn, a sign duplicates in miniature the massively elegant building that Jo and I gaze up at. This little, redundant image adds to my lingering sense of estrangement, the feeling that this trip has slipped a couple of removes from reality. Jo doesn't want to be here, even as we shift and remain. Like a chained, discontented viewer in Plato's dark cinematic cave, I can no longer take flickering shadows as truths, but out of habit keep watching anyway.

The interior of the silent Rudolfinum feels like a magnificent mausoleum. Tucked away up the double marble stairways is a photography show, with both stills and videos, sponsored by the British Council, called punnily enough, "Reality Check." It includes some half-engaging photographs by the pop star, Phil Collins. Another display, set off from the main show by hanging strips of coloured plastic, emits a nauseatingly sweet love song by Karen Carpenter. I push through the flimsy, semi-transparent doorway, and on a monitor, the head of a woman is framed by a hand-held camera. The middle-aged face is being sprayed intermittently by what looks like semen. I half-lurch out of the side-room, and walk past a male teacher who is standing in front of an installation of cleaning products, talking as fast as he can, in a high-pitched voice, to a group of pre-teens who just moments ago must have shuffled into this disturbing video—one that undercuts with harsh irony the sugary romance of the vocals. The pupils fix their eyes on the keyed-up teacher's face whose mouth issues a non-stop spiel in Czech, but no satisfactory explanation seems possible for this vile debasement of sex in which Eros becomes Thanatos. I wish I hadn't viewed this reality-check video, and I want to tell these kids that the word "love" isn't always a lie because it is sometimes.

I remember in Australia, at the Airlee Beach Bay Backpackers, how I was pulled out of sleep at a little past midnight by a woman's sharp cry of pain. Then her clear voice coming down the hall: "Leave me alone, you fucking bastard." I woke Jo up who had assimilated the sounds of anger and suffering into her dream. My back was still fragile despite an injection, so Jo got out of bed to help, maybe. I lay there, immobilized in the end room with its picturesque daytime view of the sea, hearing the manager's voice asking insistently, "Do you want me to call the police?" I heard no response. He repeated the question, but, again, no audible answer. Jo came back and reported a small group of people was there, but nothing much was going to happen. Eventually, we fell back asleep.

Why does this video installation in the Rudolfinum upset me nearly as much as that actual assault? Sexuality, I understand, brought me into this world, and is the force that vaults us over death, making a future out of our genetic past. But in this former conservatory I wished to imagine a young woman who would become my father's mother bowing lovely vibrating notes, making sounds that delight.

A Japanese name, Shizuka Yakomizo, tugs me to another display in the "Reality Check" show. Yakomizo's letter of invitation to potential subjects begins, "Dear Stranger." And his half-lit photographs offer a paradoxical semi-intimacy:

"I would like to take a photograph of you standing in your front room from the street in the evening. A camera will be set up outside your window in the street. I will not knock on your door to meet you. We must remain strangers to each other. I really hope to see you from the window. Faithfully, Artist."

Wary, yet hopeful faces peer out into the night, willing to be captured by a stranger's lens. Jo, who has been moving through the exhibits more slowly, catches up, and I ask her about the revulsive video. She said she only looked in for a moment and left. For her, a non-event. I'm relieved, but also a bit stunned: How could two people who've shared so much so well for so long react so differently?

Hope Jo will stay. I still don't want to leave Praha. Split up?

We walk over to the birthplace (now museum) of Franz Kafka—that genius of estrangement. On the way to the Old Town Square, I think of a possible parallel between him as a Jew inhabiting a mainly Czech-speaking Prague writing alienated parables in German and a sometimes-reclusive Leonard Cohen, a Jew living in francophone Montréal writing witty songs of angst in English. Jo and I trek through the old Jewish area of synagogues and cemeteries, but we both need something less gloomy.

The two of us get out the map and ride the subway to the Frank Gehry building. We stand on a corner near a bridge, look around, but see nothing. Jo and I cross the intersection, then turn back, and realize we were right under Gehry's "Ginger and Fred"! From directly below, our view had been blocked, but now the marvellous pair dances before our laughing eyes. On flexed pillars, the tall glass torso of the male leans in— with bent-arm balcony extended—towards the shorter, cylindrical, more upright partner who is swervily dressed with patches of irregularly spaced windows. She has an airy dome of unmanageable steel hair that's pale red-gold in this late light. I sense a buzz in my head of the wiry, blasted dome at Hiroshima via Ginger Rogers' hairdo, but this spinning riverfront couple is having way too much fun for that bleak association to last. Gehry's playful work in a tight space somehow fits in with the classical façades on the rest of the street. It is as if these other buildings dutifully and respectably sustain the length of workdays until the weekend when the block dances away all cares.

This evening we're off to Agharta, a jazz club not far from Wenceslas Square. Roman Pokarny, the veteran leader of this trio, is so good on guitar that he can relax into the music even as he creates it, but the night's real pleasure is listening to a young man in a tan baseball cap bearing down on a portable organ and freeing up sounds that come together rightly and newly. All this fun—homemade jazz feels needful. So we hear all three sets, and it's well after midnight before Jo and I leave, completely un-alienated. At the Alia we have to ring the night receptionist several times to let us in—like we're delinquent teenagers.

Saturday, May 3

From our window I observe a young man enter the shop opposite, come out with a tall bottle of beer, sit down on the sidewalk, his back against the storefront wall, and drink. Less than a minute later, he goes back inside with his empty, comes out with another full bottle, seats himself again on the sidewalk, back against the concrete wall, and drinks. It's like a Beckett play with the tramp-like character, the vaudeville rhythms of repetition, and a stripped-down exposure of being human.

Jo and I go for a leisurely walk, with a nervous, friendly dog joining us as our companion. Jo's funk is temporarily lifted. Putting on our packs, we set out for our last night's lodgings in Praha. Four tram/metro connections finally get us to Lipauska, where we arrive at sunny noon. Almost all the buildings here have graffiti. Jo tells me the hair on her neck tingles. We pick up a key, then are led a block away to our second floor room, which, in this dodgy area of poverty and despondency, is surprisingly large and apparently clean. But across the way is a police station, and on the corner there's a strip club, and on the facing wall are inked and painted, "NUK," "Y2K," "FUCK YOU STEALING TOY." How bad can it be?

Half-unsure, we leave behind our packs and set

out for the central post office to mail things back to Canada. But although the rest of the office is open 24 hours every day, the section that has boxes for sale is closed. Somehow, we end up back at the Rudolfinum, where we have a coffee and cake in the gallery café. Tonight in this building is a performance of Mozart's "Requiem," but we already have tickets to "Carmen." We cross the street to the Museum of Decorative Arts, which has a temporary exhibit of posters, mostly from the early 1900's. The images and fonts are colourful and enjoyable, but there's a melancholy undertow to this graphic art from our birth-century that advertises a brightly imminent future that was not only disastrous but also is now too distant even for nostalgia. Jo and I walk through the permanent exhibit of Venetian glass, shapely pieces of furniture, and exquisite fabrics, and, after "Reality Check," it is consoling to view something other than meanness, disconnection, and distress. But from the bathroom window, I look down at the old Jewish cemetery whose grey markers, under deciduous trees, are slanted by time and bitter history.

In the festive bustle of a Saturday evening, we eat dinner on the run and make our way back to the opera house, for *Carmen*. Jo and I sit in a 2nd level loge, angled down on the stage. The voices and costumes and music are all good enough, but, as Jo notes, the singer playing José isn't much of an actor, and I'd rather be at the jazz club. Afterwards, a crowded, boisterous group of soccer fans is swarming around the tram stop, waiting to catch a ride, but Jo and I manage to hop on the tram that will take us back to the Lipauska. As we step off, a mob of youths half a block away, most clutching beer bottles, starts yelling and gesturing in our direction. A woman who also got off at our stop quickens her pace. Jo and I walk briskly to our building, where a noisy party is going on in the reception area that we pass on our way up the stairs.

About 11:30 p.m., there is very loud banging and angry shouts below our window. The party gets louder until the whole building is rocking. I look out to see if the cops have shown up yet. No. Enraged voices bigger now. Noises of near-mayhem funnel up the narrow stairway, and through our thin door. Our bedroom suddenly shudders—like someone's slamming the flimsy door with a battering ram. I shove a huge armchair across the floor to wedge tight our frail door. This piece of furniture slides in so perfectly between the bathroom wall bump-out and the outer door that this must be its intended function. I go to close the curtains, but Jo would rather have them open to see what will happen next. I'm totally pumped with adrenaline, but neither fight nor flight is an immediate option. Jo says she wishes she knew the Czech language—so she could at least understand what all the yelling and violent slamming is about. I'd like to be able to talk with the unseen attackers, explain, negotiate, something . . .

From down below—every few minutes—we can now hear an alternating voice, one that is quiet and patient, trying to soothe the night beast.

But the menacing sounds of destruction persist . . .

Sunday, May 4

We wake to a calm Sunday morning. No corpses are visible down on the sidewalk. I take a shower and, when I put my pants on, discover I've been pick-pocketed. A spurt of rage, then a sag of defeat. It must have happened on the tram last night. It was so jammed with people that the driver needed several tries to get the door shut. Fortunately, it was only my "decoy" wallet, with about $30 Canadian dollars worth of korunas, and my expired membership card for the Hornby Island Blues Society. But that was most of our remaining Czech currency for this final day in Praha. The loss bothers me more than it should.

We go to the train station lockers to store our packs. To cheer me up, Jo suggests we head for John Lennon's Wall. After riding the Metro to Malá Strana, we cut through a grassy park in sudden sunshine, walk down a short side street, cross a canal, and there, sketched and painted on a water-damaged wall, are several portraits of John Lennon. In many different hands, the face of peace. The lower half of the wall is darkened by the recent flooding, but under one of the several life-like portraits of John Lennon are his still-legible words, "You may say I'm a dreamer, but I'm not the only one." Despite the Soviet authorities, protestors had scribbled impromptu messages of love.

One round painting with sun colours evokes the bright circumference of his life. Czechs, from their Prague Spring to the Velvet Revolution, have repeatedly had his courage to dream. Possessed of the imagination of lovers, they've bravely imagined diameters that extend beyond the fixed, the known, and the measurable. In homage and in remembrance of John Lennon's Montréal love-in with Yoko Ono, I write in small letters with a permanent marker pen, "We made love at Hiroshima." Jo, my beloved, always honest, says, "It feels like showing off." I'm a bit hurt, but guess she's not completely wrong.

We each buy a tiny, delicious ice cream with my not-stolen Visa card, then walk back over the Vlatava River. Near the Rudolfinum, Jo and I picnic down by the river as Ethel might have. A sensuous, circumspect, single woman of the Victorian era in a Bohemian setting, passionately wanting to become an extraordinary musician?

The Colours of a Violin

As Ethel awoke one morning from her uneasy dreams, she found on the bed the double-curved body of her violin transformed to coal-black.

She blinked twice, looked away, and then back. Her violin had returned to its normal brown. She picked it up and examined the familiar surface. Still there was the pale patch on the underside of the neck, and that long-ago scratch of unknown origins which was diagonal to the bridge. She shut the violin away in its worn leather case.

Ethel hurriedly dressed, not wanting to be late for the class. She frowned at the face in the mirror, grabbed an apple and her violin case, and went down the long hallway, through a kind of labyrinth of steps and turns and doors and passages, and emerged into uncertain sunlight. Prague was a place of riddles. She bit into the apple that tasted tart, yet winey. The Greek hawkers in Melbourne would have offered four for the price of one of these small apples. Today, she remembered, was a rehearsal of the river theme from Bedrich Smetana's "The Moldau." Now unruffled, it flowed past the grassy grounds of the Rudolfinum. Ethel discreetly tossed the half-fleshed core into a tall bush, then ran inside the half-opened door, past the double marble stairway leading upstairs, and into the large, high room.

David's bearded head tilted towards her. There was such an extra-ordinary brightness to his violin. She envied its molten sound that must be inseparable from its lacquered light. Taking out her nut-brown instrument, Ethel gave him a smile, then averted her eyes from his round face as she tuned her strings. The Professor raised his baton and the two sources of the Moldau—one warm and one cold— mingled in the sounds of two flutes, then fused as two clarinets. The movement swept the listener onward to the different watery places. David began making riverine runs on his first violin. It was a long journey marked out by Smetana: through the Bohemian countryside with its forest hunt, onto a peasant wedding, then nymphs in moonlight, next the city of Prague itself, and beyond where they now sat, the Moldau gliding north towards the ocean. (Would it be better to be a bride or a moonlit water-nymph?)

When Ethel awoke the next morning from her uneasy dreams, she found on the bed the double-curved body of her violin changed into an intense red. But when she bent over to pick it up, her violin disappeared.

She lay down again, then started up in tears. She went over to the corner of the small room and unclicked the case. On the blue felt bottom were dark ashes outlining perfectly the shape of the missing violin. On the finger pads of Ethel's left hand were whorls of fine charcoal. Yet she didn't want to leave Prague.

Violently, she shook her head, her long black hair whipping back and forth across her face. Then she caught sight of two ear-rings on the dresser top. Ethel had forgotten. She laughed and scooped up the two garnet ear-rings. Her silk dress was far too formal for a picnic, but she had nothing more appropriate. Yesterday, after rehearsal, when they were standing together on the wet grass outside the Rudolfinum, staring beyond the river, up through the mist at the Castle, David gave her the two blood-stones. Perhaps Bohemia was too alluring. Even as he dropped the two lovely ear-rings into the palm of her left hand, "in exchange," Ethel wondered how a poor student like him could afford them. David, she knew, lived in the Josefov, reputedly a place of prostitutes and thieves. In the looking-glass now, Ethel tried out a smile. She glanced down at the lace on her bodice, then raised one of her leg-o'mutton sleeves next to her frowning, oval face. When he exchanged valuables yesterday, David told her very quietly, "Garnet can turn melancholy into joy." With superstitious dread, Ethel wondered how these gems might transform someone who was not unhappy.

Fingering the tiny screw-clasp of the garnet ear-ring, she tightened it against an earlobe. The pad of flesh was both sensitive and insensitive. His hair was as black as hers. The matching one? A quick last look at who she had become, then Ethel went out through the labyrinth of steps and turns and doors and passages, side-stepping her way across the puddled streets. Ethel turned over in her mind what David had also said about his being second in the heart of the one who mattered most. She had no one else here on this continent—not even him? She heard the faint sound of strings. The broad river, swollen from last night's rain, was pushing high against its banks. David, swaying slightly, was playing a lustrous violin. Hers!

He tucked the bow under an arm, and with his slender fingers wrapped around the violin's neck began talking to her. While he spoke of how Smetana, the son of a Bohemian brewer, had solved the conundrum of how to be true to art and the world, Ethel's fingertips on her left hand started to quiver. She longed to hold her violin that had undergone such a metamorphosis. But David talked on, like the river itself.

Ethel reached up and unclasped an ear-ring. His lips kept moving—pressing and unpressing words. She removed the second garnet ear-ring, held them both out, and, at last, he halted. "In exchange, as we agreed," she said.

He touched her wrist with the back of two of his fingers that still clutched the violin. But he did not take the blood-red gems. Eyes misting, David pivoted sideways, then swung the gleaming violin back towards her—which was constantly coining new colours. It was so bright now in the sunlight that she could see her own reflection in the half-proffered instrument. Gently, he lay the newly lacquered violin on the damp paving stones. Ethel bent down by the river to pick up the lovely violin. She longed to pluck a note, but first had to free her hand of the jewelry she was squeezing. She unfolded her hand.

"Keep them, Ethel…as a memento."

"I can't, David." She dropped the garnet ear-rings into his sloping palm, one at a time. "This marvellous sheen on my violin is all I could want."

He turned away, raised a fist high into the sky, and threw the jeweled stones into the middle of the Moldau. He then ran north, along the curve of the river, the bow still tucked under his arm.

She felt a great coldness in her chest. Even the small ripples had disappeared from the surface of the water. "David!" Should she swim out and blindly dive for those tiny objects of great beauty? The river kept moving as if nothing had happened. Ethel started to run after David, that romantic fool, but paused to brush dry the smooth underside of her violin, then stopped to carefully stroke away a piece of grit that might harm the violin's lustre. No longer visible, David seemed now nearly as lost as the ear-rings. Ethel cradled the round and pointy body of her violin and walked briskly in the direction he had taken, plucking at the top string with her index finger. She then noticed a slip of paper pasted inside the violin, with a name, "Max," and an address.

Hurrying on towards the Josefov district, Ethel was determined to speak with David—this ardent young man whom she was really quite fond of. But in these shadowed, twisty, and unfamiliar streets, she was uncertain of where to go, and yearned for the open and broad and orderly lay-out of Melbourne. In this Austrian Empire of many languages, there were few Ethel encountered who could understand her Australian-accented English, but she approached a tall, white-bearded man, "Do you speak English?" He said something she couldn't grasp, that sounded like German (which she guessed might be Yiddish). Ethel pointed to the address glued inside the violin. "Max," he said, looking across the narrow street at a low doorway.

She went over and knocked, then waited. Impatient, she tried the door, which opened inward to the smell of sawdust. "Hello?" There were rasping noises, but no human voice. She took another step inside the small room, and looked around the door's edge. A large man had a small planer in his only hand. One of his hands had been severed above the wrist-bone. At his feet were wooden curls. Scrapers and gougers and clamps were neatly laid out within reach. On the work-table, two pale half-violin shapes rested, unpainted. He noticed her, but continued working as if she were not there. Pressing smoothly down on one of the arched halves, he shaved off more wood—so thinly that Ethel could see lamp-light through the fresh shavings that floated and fell through the air. She held up her shining violin.

"That belongs to a client," he said in guttural English. With his hand-less arm, he gestured to a chair.

"Oh, do you know David?"

"A *gonif*, a thief." Max scowled, and came towards her, dust in his dark hair. "And my brother. Play something."

"I have no bow."

He smiled enigmatically, and glanced

past her, at the doorway. Ethel turned to see David leaning there.

With a little flourish, he extended the bow. As Max cuffed his brother's head, Ethel began Dvorak's "Humoresque." And it was like a confirmation of a new dream as she sprang to her feet and stretched her body into the next note.

⁊

At 5:58 p.m. the train leaves for Vienna, and from there we'll make an overnight connection to Venice, that mythical city built out of salt water. Praha has yielded no answers. Only shiny fragments, half-glimpsed, below the surface.

THE STONES OF HASTINGS

grey, white, reddish-yellowish-brown, a real mixture.

Saturday, June 7

A breakfast of peaches and bread and peach tea at Fabiola and Carlotta's, then Jo and I rush out with our thanks—*grazie*. When we get to the Torino station, ten minutes before the train departs for Paris, the board says, "soppresso," cancelled, due to a rail strike in France. Frustrated travellers crush in around a harried woman at the ticket window. After waiting in a disorderly line, we speak to her with the help of a friendly guy who interprets, and she explains that another train to Paris might be running at 5 p.m., but there are no seats on it, and pushes down her small window. Suppressed.

Vaporizing our budget, we decide to take a plane to England. Jo, mainly to see good friends, is more interested in visiting this country again than I am. Dad's cousin Rob, who I'm very keen to meet, has politely let me know in a postcard that he will be too busy. Jo and I grab the first flight: Torino-Brussels-London. At the Brussels Airport, we buy some Belgian waffles and Italian wine for our hosts, Ann Vautier and Antonio Incisa Della Rocchetta. On our way to boarding the plane for the next leg of the flight, we pass a sculpture, a crouching male figure carrying a slab of Styrofoam on his back—an amusing post-modern version of Atlas. When the plane sets down at Heathrow, I feel surprisingly relaxed in this place of ex-Empire. Do I no longer carry the weight of the world on my back because I've come home to the mother country? The origin of all those English speakers that the Haidas, Hawai'ians, Maoris, and Australian aborigines never imagined on their islands?

At the Heathrow tube station, the car fills quickly and I'm conscious that our two large packs take up needed standing room. At the East Finchley Station, Jo phones Ann, and a couple of minutes later, Antonio— not waiting for a green pedestrian light—skips across in front of honking, hurtling cars to greet us. A short blond guy with a great goofy grin and jazzy energy, whose work in cognitive neuroscience is to assess the brain's loss of memory. I kid him about this being Margaret Thatcher's* constituency, and he says, "We don't talk about her." The three of us walk along the edge of a large park to Cherry Tree Road where, by their bright yellow door, Ann gives us big smiles and huge hugs. Tall and muscular, she used to play catcher—the only player who can see the whole field of play—and their house echoes this privileged perspective: a narrow building with three-story spaciousness whose garden in back looks out on high, leafy trees and the grassy expanse of the park beyond.

Jo and I re-introduce ourselves to their daughter, Caterina, who's now a lively, self-possessed girl of 12. As we chat, her parents set about preparing lamb, asparagus, and potatoes. Out of some beautiful strawberries, Antonio makes a *fragola* gelato. And, after what is probably the tastiest meal of our trip, he drives Jo and me over to Bishop's Way, where the Russian Mafia has reportedly bought up many mansions. We get out and stroll around, looking at grand, mostly vacant buildings set behind metal fences or high walls mounted with harsh security lights. A uniformed guard glares out at us. I have a foolish urge to break in. Consistent with the impulses and motives of this journey? A kind of B & E of the past—snatching at other people's belongings?

Interview with Noel Harrison at Delta, BC, November, 2002

K: Now I wanted to fill gaps in, about Betty. I remember my father sending parcels to England.

N: Yeah, that's right. Well, rather interestingly, almost for the first time, I looked up Betty on this family tree. Betty was born in 1921. Now Mother was born in 1878, something like that, no it says 74 here. Well, that means that she was 47 years old when Betty was born. Now I have to guess that it was the age factor probably that created these problems of birth for Betty that continued throughout her whole life in terms of mental deficiency. Do you know much about Betty?

K: No. As a kid, it wasn't talked about much at all. It was kind of...it was just a non-subject.

N: *Sub rosa.* But I think, I would guess that she achieved a mental age of about ten.   That's as far as she got. And she was perfectly capable of doing most things...

Sunday, June 8

After an indulgent breakfast, all five of us drive north in the Alfa Romeo to a small airport. Antonio in his pink t-shirt is flying off to France with an instructor and two other amateur pilots: an accountant and a plumber. It's a clubby sort of place with picnic tables and small aircraft. We watch Antonio take off in a blue and white plane that has Victor Alpha painted in red on its fuselage. Later, in Ann's back yard, it gets very gusty, and she frets over Antonio's flight. Jo and I are about to go look around London when the sky suddenly buckets down. Around 4:30 it clears completely and the two of us walk over to nearby Highgate Woods, then by a circuitous route over to Hampstead Heath, past Kenwood House, and pause at the viewpoint that looks south. In this very clear, late low light, Big Ben and the other landmarks are easily identifiable. But I can't find Betty anywhere.

Back at the house, I review the bits of her life I've located in the xeroxes of the *ABM Review*. As a child I had heard from my mother, by way of explanation, that Betty's head had been squeezed coming out of the womb.

1920 - "Congratulations to Mr. and Mrs. Harrison

on the birth of a daughter." A conventional phrasing that time has tinged with irony?

1924 - "The Rev. E.R. Harrison and Family"— this caption is below a photograph of Ernest, Ethel, my father, and uncle Noel, but Betty is nowhere.

1926 - "Mrs. E.R. Harrison and her three children arrived from Japan per s.s. 'Tanda,' on 26th December, en route to Melbourne, where the children will go to school."

1929 - "Mrs. E.R. Harrison, with her daughter, left at the end of May on her return journey to Japan."

1931 - "The Rev. E.R. Harrison writes from Chiba, Japan:

One thing which rather makes us hesitate is that the winter climate up there [Akita] is rather severe, and as our little girl has been very delicate we must find out what the effect is likely to be. As far as we are concerned, we are prepared to go anywhere, but it is only right that the question of the child's health should be fully considered."

This last passage is as near as the correspondence comes to hinting at anguish over their daughter. And it reads more like loving someone a lot.

Antonio returns safely from France, and the four

adults have a late supper of risotto, and two bottles of red wine—both from Veneto and with the same year on the labels: one was already in the house; the other we've just brought from Belgium. Carl Jung is sometimes right about synchronicity. Antonio had no weather problems during the flight, and after dinner he shows us a few minutes of video he shot coming into the French coast. We go to the living room, where Antonio puts on a zydeco tape. I like how the double-stopping of the fiddle creates interesting little discords, and how this music of French-Canadians exiled long ago to Louisiana matters to my Italian pal in London.

Monday, June 9

I wake up early to start revising for electronic publication the conference paper on *The Tempest* I gave in Hawai'i, where this long journey began. I sit, staring at my words on Ann's screen:

> *"...the innocent Miranda versus the ignorant Caliban. If, as I argue here, these judgements can be reversed, what remains notable is a shared vulnerability to illusion."*

Where would Betty fit? Which adjective, "innocent" or "ignorant," would be truer?

Jo and I take the Northern Line down to Embankment Station, cross Hungerford Footbridge, and walk west along the Thames to the London Eye, a gigantic revolving wheel with glassy capsules. Jo likes it but I half-resist its charm, worry about Disneyfication— the conversion of this city into a viewable theme park. But, then again, 400 years ago, there was a massively popular "eye" that transformed the whole world into a viewable theme park: Shakespeare's Globe Theatre.

The Saatchi Gallery has an exhibit on Dali. Earlier in my life I wouldn't have missed it, but now, too much melted time gone by? We walk on, widdershins, east along the broad blue-grey river, slowing at the

Tate Modern Gallery whose huge swaying balloon figure seems to shout out, "We're not stodgy!" Jo and I continue on to the reconstructed Globe, located 200 yards away from its original site. An approximate past as exact as you can get on this spinning earth? The woman guide, in an engaging mini-performance, describes Shakespeare's theatre as a jewelbox with a plain outside and a richly painted interior—could double as a description of the man himself? The rebuilt Globe, pegged together from 100-year old oak, has the only thatch roof permitted in London since the Great Fire. Inside, Jo and I examine the hand-sewn, gold-threaded costumes, listen to the thunder of cannon balls crashing down the enclosed ramp with its wooden bumps, and then enter the theatre itself.

A huge metal slide dominates the thrust stage, and an arched ladder in stainless steel is part of this playground. The set echoes the playfulness of the city outside with its giant Ferris Wheel Eye and the Tate's inflated, three-dimensional cartoon. Jo and I sit in a lower gallery and watch a little-known work, Christopher Marlowe's *Dido, Queen of Carthage*, in rehearsal. The director asks the actors for subtle changes in voice and movement, and they respond fluently. The play takes as its initiating context the burnt towers of Troy, thus fitting within the year's theme of Regime Change—and makes a sidelong allusion to the destroyed Twin Towers that led to the invasion of Iraq? There are some parallels too, perhaps, in Aeneas's travels to North Africa, where he ultimately abandons his commitment, to his lover, Dido. I become aware of Jo, to my right, sneaking photos. Several elusive political analogies to sort out, but I set them aside, unclarified. Again I'm struck by the paradox that actors (like novelists?) are most alive when pretending to be someone else. Everyone must want to leap beyond the one life they get. Do roles give us a few hours of relief from whoever we are or, by inhabiting several, do we become fully human?

Outside, the sunlight lights up the river. Jo wants to visit the Design Museum, that's a bit further east. The first exhibit offers us a small homecoming, since the best fifty chairs of the last hundred years makes tangible those imaged on a framed poster in our bathroom on Hornby Island. A second exhibit traces the evolving design of Mac computers, but what it really shows is the astonishing rate at which an agitated profit motive jettisons what's bright fun and advanced technological function for consumer nextness. The third exhibit reverses directions, demonstrating how an artist can use contemporary materials to recreate what's considered *passé*, in this case, the aesthetic of the baroque. It's reassuring to know I'm not the only one trying to retrieve ghostly forms.

Near London Bridge, Jo and I catch the tube "home" for a pasta dinner, with Antonio cooking for everyone again. After the clean-up, I ask him—in between the astonishing percussive riffs he forms in his mouth—if he'd read aloud part of the *Inferno*. Antonio sprints upstairs and comes back down in a minute with a small, aged volume. Five weeks in Italy have tuned my ears into Italian a little, but I'm grateful when he stops to translate the music of these lines. In their concern with human evil, these cantos have such a melancholy beauty that I'm reminded that Primo Levi was able to trade a recital of these words for bread in Auschwitz. Here, now, listening to Dante's poetry about Hell on a give-y couch, a brandy glass in hand, with my beloved and our friends, is likely as close as I'm going to get to *Paradiso*.

Was my aunt Betty happy or unhappy? Might her child-like "presentness" have freed her from regrets and worries, from both the past and future? Did she feel abandoned when Ernest's sister, Nell (the nurse), who was caring for her, died, and Betty briefly ended up in institutional care? Ethel, her widowed mother, definitely was not at peace with that situation. The adventuresome student in Prague, the talented violinist in Melbourne, the romantic traveller to Japan, had, in far-off Canada, become anxious about her faraway daughter's well-being.

Letter to Mrs. Ethel Harrison from Dr. J. V. Morris,

Medical Superintendent, Norfolk County Council

3rd June, 1946

Dear Madam,

Betty Harrison

With regard to your enquiries about Betty. She is quite incapable of earning her living as a maid, and no matter how well intended the Nursing Home, her employment there would be nothing more than sweating labour, and I feel that she would be back in the Colony in a very short time.

Secondly, I have no objection whatever to her going anywhere else, but I would commend you to consider the fact that it would be once again a disturbance, and that no form of psychological treatment is likely to improve Betty's condition which arises from a primary defect. If the girls in this Home which you suggest are mal-adjusted girls, you will of course realize that Betty will once again be suffering a psychological disadvantage and will quite probably be unhappy, and the change having once been effected, it would be unreasonable to expect my Committee to allot her another vacancy. In other words, if she goes from here, she stays away from here; as I cannot accept responsibility for either suggestions.

To the best of my knowledge and Matron's, Betty is normally perfectly happy and contented, but her holidays have a considerable up-setting effect upon her, in so far as she has been asked and offered a job. You will realize that the labour situation in this Country is so bad that people are employing assistance, no matter how inefficient; and I feel that your friends and Betty's, by insisting on this question of a job will do more harm than good for your daughter.

Might I suggest that you write to Betty and advise her to settle down and be contented.

Tuesday, June 10

We wake up to iffy weather, but Ann, Jo, and I decide to drive off anyway to Sissinghurst Garden. When we finally get out the door, Ann finds out she has locked her keys in the boot. We have a latté in her garden and hash out Plan B.

Jo and I take the tube to downtown London, explore a bit under a misty sky, and then head back to the Globe for a performance of *Richard II*. In the drizzle by the sullen Thames, Jo and I wolf down some sandwiches as the bell rings. We enter the wooden O to trumpet music from the galleries high above the stage, and the beginning of the Wars of the Roses begins. The play feels slowish, but Mark Rylance's performance as the poet king keeps spurring the production forward. Jo gives up her covered seat, and slips down to the ground floor to watch the action close-up, her elbows propped high on the front of the stage. The arrival of the late afternoon sun through the open rooftop brings an incongruously festive mood to the crowd, even as we watch, helpless, as King Richard II, a human capable of wit, delight, eloquence, irony, and (even) insight, is deposed. The aggressive, single-minded figure who will become King Henry IV is like a prototype for George W. Bush who will several centuries later defeat in the presidential election a wordy and well-meaning and ineffectual Al Gore, a Richard II clone? Faces in the audience are smiling at this enactment of tragedy, but not at the relevant world outside.

At the interval, I join Jo as a groundling on the tamped-down, permeable floor that's made up, in part, of hazelnut shells. When the performance comes to an end, there's much clapping in rhythm as the company dances an intricate jig instead of taking a bow. Everyone has had a good time watching a representation of suffering. Shakespeare in his epic, eight-play history of the Wars of the Roses only uses the word, "tragedy," twice on the title pages, for this very first work and the very last one, about the villainous *Richard III*. It is as if everything in between the beginning and end of the 86-year long civil war is normal, an extended comedy.

Why is the world always shocked by the outbreak of war when killing each other in large numbers seems to be a human constant? At least two of my missionary grandfather's six brothers fought in the Great War: Lance Corporal Robert J. Harrison, nickname "Bert," of 1st Canadian Mounted Rifles, was killed at Ypres, 6th of June 1916, and Frederick who, Noel says, "was in World War I, and he was pretty badly wounded, and changed by that." Frederick was the father of "Cousin Rob," who doesn't want to meet me.

At the inquest into Frederick Harrison's death, Harry George Harrison, a chemist living in London, stated that

> "his brother served in the Royal Garrison Artillery from March 17, to September, 1919, serving on the Italian, Mesopotamian, Egyptian and Salonikan fronts in the rank of

a bombardier. During the time he served in war he contracted malaria, and after that he was a totally different man." *Cambridge Daily News* Tuesday, July 5, 1927

The theme of war runs through the lives of almost all of my male ancestors. Glued onto cheap, easily torn paper in a tall book with a dark green cover titled "Scraps" is a newspaper article Dad wrote in 1939, "Students Honour Great War Dead," just as another world war began—one in which he would soon serve in Coastal Command, ditching a plane off the Queen Charlotte Islands.

Students Honour Great War Dead

(by John Harrison)

The Hamilton Spectator, September, 1939

Present Conflict Stresses Sacrifices Made on

Flander's Fields

With the ending of the peace of the 1918 era the British Empire finds itself involved in the toils of war once more, and, with a clearer realization than ever before of the true meaning of war, school children throughout Hamilton paid tribute to-day to those who fell in the years 1914-1918.

As the children observed the two minutes' silence the significance of the occasion was brought home to them with a new and added intensity, for on this Memorial day they, their families and those who were dear to them were the people who might be called upon to make the sacrifice rather than dim-remembered heroes who died 20 or more years ago.

On this occasion they were more firmly impressed with the horror and futility of war, but they realized that if they were to live in a free world certain existing evils must be wiped out. As they listened to addresses on the meaning of Armistice and heard the words of In Flanders Fields they echoed the sentiments of the words:

"At the going down of the sun, and in the morning,

We will remember them."

Wednesday, June 11

I wake up, and spend nearly six hours revising the *Tempest* paper I wrote months ago. Fighting both the deadline and the prose I once liked:

> "Prospero's language, particularly the use of the word, 'companions,' implies that Caliban, despite cultural variegation, is akin to the humans in the trio, and not a 'monster.' As well, Prospero softens his earlier reference to Caliban as a born devil, now merely calling him a 'demi-devil,' a description which could include all of flawed humanity. Finally, and most importantly, Prospero acknowledges his own sins through a line break that acts as a kind of self-confession, linking himself to Caliban, the black sheep of the family: 'this thing of darkness I / Acknowledge mine.'
>
> "His acceptance of Caliban as a fellow human breaks the mental construct of colonialism, with its self-aggrandizing and xenophobic categories of gods and monsters. At the end of *The Tempest*, Prospero, like Caliban, has seen through the cross-cultural mirages that still entrap Miranda . . ."

You breathe the air even if it's toxic. Race and racism. As a kid on some beach or sidewalk or playground, I learned the word, "retard." I enter the revisions on Ann's Mac, and think about the ending:

> "Prospero and Caliban converge from the opposing categories of the divine and the bestial, and both metamorphose into human beings. They are the only two characters within the play who achieve a full interiority. The wise, compassionate leader understanding pragmatic limits and the articulate native son seeking a rightful heritage become clear-sighted counterparts. History, I suggest, offers us a tangible glimpse of what occurs when these two transformed figures became one: Nelson Mandela."

At these moments of composing sentences, do I re-enact my father or my grandfather? Neither? Both were journalists—not profs or novelists—and their writings had to cope with a daily-ness of deadlines:

> "Whilst under my direction, Mr. [Ernest] Harrison was required to undertake not only a great variety of reporting work—from police court cases to assizes to County Council meetings, and from village sports to university first-class fixtures—but also to lend a hand in the sub-editing of country correspondents' 'copy,' the getting out of 'reprint,' and the reading of proofs. He was also encouraged to

supply notes, &c., for the numerous 'special' columns which at that time formed a marked feature in the 'Cambridge Express,' of which I was then the Editor, and further, to contribute occasional original articles.

"He can take a good Shorthand Note or write a smart paragraph.

"Mr. Harrison's social qualifications are of the highest order. Gentlemanly, steady, of good address, and reliable, he may be trusted to be a credit to his paper wherever he goes . . . ."

A. R. Hill, F. J. I.   March 30, 1905

Am I going to find time to check out Ethel's birthplace and family records in Croydon? "Mercer" means one who deals in textiles, so it's no wonder I'm comfortable with "the woven"—*textus*—and as a fiction writer sometimes make up things out of the whole cloth. Yet the autobiographical self, too, is engaged in "making up"—not only through mythologizing the past but also perhaps in trying to arrive at a peaceable settlement with family history.

In mid-afternoon, instead of going to Croydon, I too easily accept Ann's offer to drive Jo and me over to Fenton House, which is sited on a nearby height of land. Along with a display of historic musical instruments, there is an exhibit of movie costumes that includes the long, soft, Harris Tweed coat from *Withnail and I*, the cult drinking film, and some fancy garb from a recent production of Jane Austen's *Mansfield Park*. Outside, in

227

the garden of Fenton House, under shifting clouds, it is both dark and luminous—like these two contrastive works of the English imagination.

For dinner, Ann makes a Japanese mackerel dish, with rice, beans, and fennel, but she's not impressed by the fish itself. Antonio, to everyone's amusement, keeps echoing her phrase, "Hang on, please." At about 11 p.m. he and I walk out to shop and, at my prompting, Antonio talks about categories of knowledge and memory. The brain, he says, tends to lose nouns before verbs, maybe because actions are part of the motor pathway. One of his patients, an engineering prof, can remember only maps. Another man can recall "vacuum cleaner," but not "bumblebee." Sadness lurks in our heads.

Where does the truth lie, in both senses of that word? Names, places, dates can get dizzying. At the death of Nell—did Ethel, an ocean and a continent away in Vancouver—arrange for the return from Africa of Ernest's niece, Dorothy, to help care for Betty?

As Prospero says, "I / Acknowledge mine."

Interview with Noel Harrison at Delta, BC,
November, 2002

N: And then when Nell died, I guess, Betty was taken care of by County Council for a very short period of time until Dorothy, who had worked for some time in Africa in the Wantage sisterhood, had come back to England and made arrangements for Betty to work and live with the sisters. The sisterhood in England, I think, was dealing very substantially with geriatric cases and she sort of worked in these homes, just being very useful but being taken under the auspices of that sisterhood, you know.

K: Sounds like wonderful usefulness in two directions.

N: It worked out extremely, yeah. She could work with them and she enjoyed that work and I saw her twice during the war when I was over there, and subsequently I went back on business trips on three, four, or five occasions. I would see her each time just to say hello. But when I did see her, she said it was great to see you again kind of stuff, all that sort of thing, and at the end of that luncheon, we'd stroll through the village streets nearby and I'd go my way and she'd go her way.

. . .

N: Your father John went to England only once, just prior to her death

K: Yes, yes.

N: And he saw Betty I think every day he was there. He was in London but he would take the train out there. Betty had been ill while he was there and he had seen her essentially in hospital. She had cancer, and was running down in health.

Thursday, June 12

Jo and I take the Northern Line down to Waterloo Station to get Eurostar tickets for Paris, but after at least 20 minutes at the counter, Jo receives only duplicate tickets to trade in for the real tickets when we leave London. We go on to Oxford Circus via Charing Cross, and at McDonald's I mistakenly order a children's portion. After walking over to Marylebone High Street and checking out the Conran shop, we end up in Regent's Park. In Queen Mary's Garden are roses and roses and more roses. By a waterfall, a brown duckling above a rocky ledge tries to make its way back down to the pond, hesitates, and fails, over and over again. At last, it slides abruptly down into the water— that it now can't climb back up out of! It's agonizing to watch its again-and-again attempts to scale the slippery vertical rock, straining to get back to where, just moments ago, it didn't want to be.

We take the tube to Leicester Square to visit the National Portrait Gallery. Here, where the subject's name comes first, art often finishes second—though many works reveal a charged, sometimes quirky connection between the sitter and the artist. The face of David Beckham possesses an unadvertised menace in the dark, cool eyes that have usefully limited the world to what they can exploit. The Chandos painting of

Shakespeare, next to an opened door, is more intensely present than I remember. The past, it seems, keeps twisting its shape. Like a fallen arbutus branch—heated by the sun, washed in rain, half-hidden under snow, misted by fog—it won't keep still. Looking this time at Shakespeare's observant, half-amused face, I sense he's considering going for a drink with you, but there's some writing to be done, in fact, both a comedy and a tragedy, so not today. Jo and I forego the Victorian portraits, and hurry back to Regent's Park to watch his early comedy, *Two Gentlemen of Verona*.

Miniature houses on tall poles in back of the stage represent Verona. Visually, it's fun, but Jo thinks the birdhouse-effect will diminish the imagined lives. Stage right and left are open sweeps of grass that let ticket-holders get to their seats, and allow the cast to make their entrances and exits. The start of the play is irritating for us because the actor playing Proteus doesn't project his voice strongly enough into the cool evening air, and yobs sitting in the row behind us—lured to Shakespeare in the park by bottles in picnic baskets and girlfriends' intimations of fun?—pursue their own drunken dialogue, kidnapping the nearby audience. Jo and I move our seats, only to end up beside a woman who throughout the entire first half of play talks without pausing to a friend who never once answers, or alters her forward profile. Is it just us ex-colonials who still care about how Shakespeare's lines let us imagine ourselves? On stage, the only laughter generated before the break is via the sometimes witty joking of the two player servants and the shambling entrance of a lurcher.

For the second half, Jo and I shift down closer

to the actors, and the performance seems to pick up. With a mix of refined poetry and gross humour (a piss-off remark involving the dog), Shakespeare's play should appeal to diverse play-goers, but the repetitive moments of language betray a fear that the audience might not get it—or maybe won't be listening…to a romantic comedy that comes across as mostly unlovely and unfunny. The inability of the actors to make their lines work is agonizing to watch, like the duckling's desperate again-and-again attempts to scale the steep rock-face. After the clumsily imposed happy ending of *Two Gentlemen of Verona*, tension remains: Will the dog at the curtain-less curtain call respond to its command? It does, and the lurcher gets the evening's biggest round of applause. It has to be tough on an actor when your efforts and talent don't matter. That risk of failure, part of any performance of self?

Friday, June 13

Out of a nearly endless London, Ann, Jo, and I drive off in the Alfa Romeo towards Sissinghurst Castle Garden. Slowly, the hilly countryside of East Sussex emerges. Ann volunteers to drop me off at Hastings, where Aunt Betty spent a period of her life—I could take the train back, but I decline with thanks. I'll likely go there in a few days, perhaps on Sunday. At Sissinghurst, the first thing I notice is the actual press of Hogarth Press—the one on which Virginia and Leonard Woolf typeset *The Waste Land*. With its big toothy wheel, the shiny brass connecting rods, a flat seat-like board, and the roller positioned like a handlebar, the machine appears to be a prototype for a motorcycle. T. S. Eliot's words about an unreal city with falling towers bursting in the violet air roar off, careen into a New York future.

The neo-classical design of the boxed hedge yews hem in and open out perspectives—and provide for shade on this very hot day. Jo and I climb up the steep inner stairs to a high flat rooftop and look down on the geometry of flowerbeds. Ann stands on the bright lawn below, pointing our camera upward. At Jo's suggestion, the two of us stand on opposite sides of the brick tower, which has an eight-sided conical cap and a black weather vane that projects dozens of feet above our heads. We gesture down at our friend—jokily signify our separateness. Yet even in this act of mutual clowning, there is a truth about human apartness. After we descend, I'm happy to learn Jo and I at least waved with complementary hands.

The three of us drive on to the gardens at Great Dixter, which are crowded and luxuriant—uncountable plant varieties here. In their studied casualness, these gardens helped define an English aesthetic ideal: a joining of the poetic and the prosaic. (A model as well for a kind of travel writing?) We go inside a building from the Tudor period, where an elderly woman with a very sharp mind details its social history, telling us how upper and lower classes shared the large main room with its High Table. The floor at the far end, upon which a long table rests, is raised slightly to create a shallow stage. The drama of inequality continues in the next room where I notice someone—a carpenter?—has carved his commonplace name into one of the massive ceiling beams, in a spidery hand, "John Harrison," then incised a date from the reign of Queen Elizabeth I.

Outside in the colourful, scented profusion of the gardens of Great Dixter, the three of us enjoy ice creams and a ginger beer. But a phone call from Antonio interrupts our leisure. His *bête noir* boss has just set up for the coming Tuesday an ominous meeting. Ann drives us back to London, where we buy some fruit and wine. Antonio makes us all a pasta supper, then he and I stay up to watch *The Sopranos*—a lengthy episode. The two of us don't move towards bed until 1 a.m., with the unspoken kinship of fatigue.

Saturday, June 14

Ann shows me the four red clay tennis courts at the end of their block, and I want to live here! After breakfast, the four adults follow Caterina to her school for a fund-raising fete, which has on sale lots of books worth reading. The morning is sunny fun with games and raffles and barbecues and beer and balding dads in a ragged rock band playing with gusto inappropriate songs for pre-teens, such as "Let's Get It On" and "Brown Sugar": overt sexual invitation and Mexican heroin? Yet the atmosphere is totally benign, with the amateur performers likely more innocent than their half-bored, half-embarrassed sons and daughters waiting for the stage to be cleared. A rock band of 13 or 14 year olds comes on, and their gifted lead guitarist does a dramatic split-kick—a startling contrast to the older guy who occasionally thumped his left foot. It is a nice community to be almost part of for a few hours. Against the hostile Brit stereotype, there's abundant laughter and not a stiff upper lip in the bunch.

Jo and I decide to catch the tube south, and walk along the Strand, where a demo is in progress. A black man speaks fervently against the mis-rule of Robert Mugabe—the ex-colony of Rhodesia obviously is not so lucky in its leadership as South Africa was. We walk on to Somerset House, where kids on this very hot day run through multiple little "fountains" on a large open square. Inside is a photo exhibit of snow and St. Petersburg, drawn from the Hermitage Museum. There are also striking studio shots of ordinary people carrying various loads on their backs—such as heavy stacks of wood. Juxtaposed to these smiling, Atlas-like images are photographs of the hyper-privileged in elaborate costumes at dress-up balls. The date for one of these precedes the Little Russian Revolution of 1905 by a mere two years, but there is no mention here of that Bloody Sunday in St. Petersburg when troops fired on unarmed workers led by a priest who wanted to give a petition to Czar Nicholas II at his Winter Palace.

Jo and I once more cross the sunshiny square, to the Courtauld Institute. Great Manets here, including the barmaid who's seen too much. Monet's vased flowers look gorgeous even from across the room, doing in any critical detachment, and up close I read his angled signature that's in the same red as the brightest of the petal flecks. Nearby are the greens Cézanne's palette knife slapped on so precisely they've become pure chlorophyll. Two Gaugins, large, cool, and mysterious. It's a punch in the chest to see the first painting Van Gogh made after slicing off his ear: his eyes look unflinchingly at the man he has just become. I'm about to contemplate the Modigliani nude when in comes Antonio, who casually says, "Hi."

A miscommunication at the school fair—he had wanted to come with us to the St. Petersburg retrospective. I'm touched that he's bothered to track us down. The three of us have a coffee by the Thames, then Antonio asks if he can show us a painting. We say sure, and he leads Jo and me to the London Gallery, whose free admission policy allows us to drop in exactly like this. We go up the stairs, and there's Holbein's *The Ambassadors*. I have photographic copies of this commanding double portrait in books, but here is the outsize thing itself, full frontal. Having just come from the Courtauld's Impressionist masterpieces, I'm struck by the physical solidity of these two painted men. But under Antonio's guidance, I take a sideline view of the canvas, and some meaningless coloured lines in the foreground come into startling focus: an anamorphic skull.

Back at Cherry Tree Road, Ann has a salad and cold cut dinner waiting for us. Afterwards, Antonio, Jo, and I walk over to the local repertory movie theatre—the oldest independent one in Britain—that's showing a re-release of *The Leopard* (1963), with Burt Lancaster. Adapted by Luchino Visconti from the novel, *Il Gattopardo*, the film has a strong story shape with every scene adding a plot element, usually unpredictably so. The sexy young lovers (Alain Delon and Claudia Cardinale) play hide and seek in the empty, dilapidated rooms of an enormous building, and, at the interval, Antonio—a Count somehow related to Pope Alexander VII—says he's pretty sure some of the interior scenes were filmed at his family's place (before his cousin who went to help the starving in China sold the property for very little). The second part of this three-hour film has a dream-like ballroom scene whose duration nearly lasts like real time. Unlike with the St. Petersburg photos, here you intimately feel the splendour and decay of an aristocratic world. The stylish cinematic images of a camera that never ceases its motion and the poignant happiness of the strings render the dancing bodies elegiacally. "One of the films I live by," avers Martin Scorsese, whose stories of bravado, intensity, and gore seem to have zero time for nostalgia, but, in their speeded-up frames, share Visconti's sense of the fleeting and the vulnerable. I want the rapt dancers in their exquisite clothes to glide through the shining frames of *The Leopard* forever. But in contrast to our near-infinite human desires, life-spans are finite. It is that chasm that both haunts and enlivens us, and **it is** where art comes from.

Although Death, that boogeyman around the next corner, saves us from blandness and boredom, it is, for the most part, unwelcome. And when Death takes the form of killing, it inflicts more than a physical ending. Even though it concerned quite distant relatives, I was staggered to hear from Noel of murder in our family history:

"Well, anyway Fred killed his wife [Florence] and child [Geoffrey, 17] who were both at home, and then he committed suicide himself. Rob [12] was not at home; otherwise he might well have been done away with too, but anyway that's something that happened a long time ago. I think it was Rob finally who gave us the full picture on that, as much as it was given."

In old newspapers, there are more morbid and melodramatic details. Including a horrifying, brave, first-person account by "Bobbie," Dad's cousin Rob.

"Lying on the table before the Coroner was the double barrelled sporting gun which had played such a terrible part in the awful calamity. The Coroner had hoped to save the younger son the ordeal of giving evidence, but, when sworn, he proved a bright lad of exceptional intelligence."

St. Neots Post July 7, 1927

"I went into the dining room and Dad came in and asked me to fetch a pint of milk from Mr. Noble, in Green-street. Dad came down the yard with me. He said 'Don't come in the backway when you come back; come in by the front door.'"

"The Coroner: Did you go in by the backway?"

"Witness: Yes; when I fetched the milk."

"Just as I got to the gate, which was slightly open, I saw Geoff, lying by the side of his cycle, with part of his head missing, and a large quantity of blood about. I shouted out for help, and came towards the house calling "mum,' and then saw Dad lying on the ground with part of his head blown away, and a double barrelled gun lying beside him. I ran into the house and also saw mother

241

lying on the floor with her head partly blown away, a great quantity of blood, and her brains lying on the floor. I ran to my auntie (Mrs. Weston) and told her what I had seen...

The Huntingdonshire Post July 7, 1927

Sunday, June 15

I wake up early to take the train to Hastings, but can't break out of the house. All the exits are locked and no keys are visible. Ann told us about a neighbour whose keys were extracted through the mailbox by a magnet at the end of a fishing rod. Luckily, Ann comes down the stairs just now, and also phones the train station—very usefully as I'd forgotten the train for Hastings left from Charing Cross. I half-hope to attend an 11 a.m. Anglican service in Hastings, and perhaps later find out some of the history of Betty Harrison's life and work and "illness." I catch the 10:10 out of London that's crowded and noisy with fussing babies, so instead of reading a book, I pick up a discarded tabloid. A large image of David Beckham on the cover, a marital/fashion story half-way through, and, of course, another photo of the footballer in the sports section at back. Most of England, it seems, lives gladly in his iconic shadow. Betty, her face half-hidden, a very different figure.

At Hastings I get off the train, and spot an ad for a combination ticket for the railway and admission to the famous battlefield. Impulsively, I buy a ticket, then rush to board a train that's just leaving—six and a half miles back the way I've just come. After a few intervening stops, at a sign for Battle with crossed swords, I step down off the train and walk up the hill towards a stone building, an Anglican church. I'm taking some photos when a friendly, bearded guy by the open front doors tells me there'll be a harpsichord recital at two. The timing might work out. Walking on to the small town, I go underneath an arched entrance that's between high, twin octagonal towers, and into the Abbey and its battlefield. The imposing, fortified abbey was erected by the Norman conqueror in gratitude to God for his victory.

On headphones, three separate voices relate the battle of 1066: a Norman, a Saxon, and Harold's mistress, Edith Swan-Neck. It takes a sophisticated, psychologically sure culture to be able to offer multiple and clashing viewpoints of such a crowning (and un-crowning) moment of national self-definition—the French take-over of England's throne. Most states can't admit the many-sidedness of history.

Walking on, I find myself alone in a smaller abbey with marble pillars. A pale golden light suffuses everything here. I'm in no hurry to leave. But other visitors come in, and I go outside, onto the narrow ridge that the Saxons defended against William the Conqueror's invading army until an arrow pierced Harold's eye. Today, on the sunny green battlefield, people are picnicking. In 1944, Canadian troops were stationed here, waiting to invade Normandy.

I'm too late for the harpsichord recital. I walk downhill to the Battle train station where, at the last moment, I realize I'm on the wrong side of the tracks— and hustle across the overpass. The train returns me to the town of Hastings itself, to salt air and the cry of gulls. Was Betty a swimmer? I can't imagine she ever used one of those fancy bathing machines seen in the historical pictures—white-and-blue striped canvass on high iron wheels. But it's nice to know she, too, lived near the ocean for much of her life, listening to the moon tug at the sea, then let go. I walk along the strand with its large pebbles: grey, white, reddish-yellowish-brown, a real mixture. There are shouts from the beach and cameras are lifted in front of faces as a rowing race nears the finish line by the pier. In the 1400's, sea raiders from France burnt Hastings to the ground, and the century before that tides and heavy winds washed away much of the town. Now it's a happy festive scene with bikinis and sunburst tattoos as three contending boats of rowers surge forward, past the outstretched pier. I pick up a smooth grey stone that pleases me, then a pitted yellow-brown one that feels true. Pocketing them, I buy an ice cream that I eat slowly. An immense amount I'll never know.

With the sea on my right and a high cliff to the left, I walk east, towards a beach-launched fleet. The tall net lofts have "clinker-style," overlapping horizontal boards, like a boat's wooden hull, to keep the water out. Attracted by a shop that says "Hastings Rock," I go inside, hoping to find some curious geological specimen. But there are only touristy gifts and cards—several with images of that pseudo-Ojibway, Grey Owl, who was born in this town as Archibald Belaney. He grew up with aunts and a grandmother here on England's south coast before sailing off to Canada to begin his off-stage impersonation of an Indian, a feat discovered only after his death. Hastings Rock turns out to be a hard candy stick, either mint or fruit. I buy one—apparently a tradition for day-trippers. The owner tells me the long pier that was the finish line in the race also marks the otherwise invisible transition from Hastings to St. Leonards-on-Sea, where "cousin Rob" lives.

The postcard he sent mentioned that, apart from Noel and a cousin Monica in Sweden, he's probably the only one left from my father's generation. Is it somehow symbolic that I can't even find the information centre here in Hastings? What I really want to get is an interior sense of who Betty was. Ernest and Ethel and Dad left behind inked words from which I might discern their inner worlds, but I can't read what my aunt left unwritten.

I cross over a non-boundary into St Leonards-on-Sea. An ornate church, erected in the vee of two streets, confronts me. On its large, highly decorative fountain is a plaque:

"Jesus said whosoever drinketh of this water shall thirst again. But whosoever drinketh of the water that I shall give him shall never thirst."

"Erected 1861 by subscription by the inhabitants of Hastings and St Leonard including the pence of children . . ."

I take a sip, then wander around some more. Two mysterious relatives, my father's sister and his cousin Rob, inhabited, at slightly different times, this more or less shared space, separated only by an imaginary line. In his note to me, Dad's cousin Rob wasn't unfriendly, just, understandably, self-protective. There's a distinction between a relative and a stranger that I could exploit, but I don't want to intrude. *His father Fred was in World War I, and he was pretty badly wounded, and changed by that.* A different kind of casualty than Rob and Dad's uncle Bert, whose life was erased at what the soldiers called Wipers (Ypres). I buy a few historical booklets about Hastings, then board the train for London. I lack the ice of a good reporter who gets the whole disturbing story.

Frederick Harrison, who took over the family butcher business, it seems, was worried about finances. An active member of the St. Ives Rowing Club, the driver of a motorcycle with a sidecar, and a long-time Conservative, Fred was also, according to sworn testimony at the inquest, "A very cheerful man." What made him spare Bobbie, and not his other son? In the midst of homicidal craziness, he knew through some kind of mad lucidity that his unusually able younger son could survive this horror. *The Secret Life of Us.*

If I had known of this ancestral family violence, could I have written about the brutal murder of Pat Lowther by her husband? Oddly, the parallel might have made me too conscious of familial echoes: I might not have listened so closely to another's story, and not have gained the trust and ongoing friendships of her daughters. But I have to wonder about the easy rapport I once felt in Leclerc Penitentiary with thieves, drug-dealers, and murderers when I taught there—one course was titled "Metamorphosis." I think, too, about my great grandparents who had two daughters and seven sons, and how that sense of plenty must have suddenly withered.

> Much sympathy is felt for Mr. and Mrs. William S. Harrison in the terrible tragedy. Mr. Harrison, sen., who was Mayor of St. Ives 1915-16-17, lost one son in the war. He also lost his eldest son, a very promising solicitor in the town, some two years ago.

Cambridge Daily News July 5, 1927

Mostly, though, I want to know how Dad's cousin Rob stared into the blackest abyss, and flew beyond.

At London, I transfer from the train to the tube, and ride towards my wife and friends.

He refused to quit. Like that never-say-die Hiroshima eucalypt, Cousin Rob became a navigator during the war (as did my father). A role akin to Kafka's land surveyor? Ultimately, "Bobbie" was promoted to Wing Commander. On leaving the RAF, he bought into a failing stationery business, resuscitated it with great success, and retired early. Uncle Noel told me his cousin Rob had a much loved wife, Doris, and that the couple raised two happy children. Somehow he managed to shape a life unconfused by pain.

At the garden picnic table, Jo tells me of her wanderings today through London parks, and, as we wait for Ann and Antonio to get back from their day-long outing, we eat tomato and bacon sandwiches. Even as I'm enjoying this simple meal, I have an impulse to become a vegan, but then think about our family tradition (on both sides), one made explicit in a St. Ivian reminiscence of my great-grandfather:

> In the early dawn of Monday markets he could be seen carefully feeling the firm sides of fat bullocks. It seemed to me nobody could choose their beef better and more carefully than Mr. [William Sparrow] Harrison, and as my mother dealt with him the scene was more interesting, in view of appetizing beef steak puddings and prime Sunday joints to come.

The *Huntingdonshire Post* July 7, 1927

Though a convert to the Church of England about the time his son, Ernest, went to Cambridge University to study theology, both he and his wife, Emily Reed, my great-grandmother, are buried in a Quaker cemetery. I'm glad to be linked to a religion associated with the abolition of slavery and protests of conscience against war—even if "Quaker butcher" sounds like a contradiction in terms.

In St. Ives, a town of non-Conformist tendencies (with its prominent statue in the high road of a one-time resident, Oliver Cromwell), two of Dad's other cousins fought hard and well to keep England's huge motorway out. Its wide, busy pavement that now bypasses the town has a section on the outskirts called Harrison Way. (Is there a Harrison way?)

About 10 p.m. Ann and Antonio and Caterina

come home from Chichester. I give Caterina the fruit-flavoured stick of Hastings rock, and when she smiles, Ann says it can be part of her school lunch tomorrow. The four of us adults stay up, eating cheese and crackers and drinking red wine from the Rhone valley, enjoying a last late evening chat.

Tomorrow morning, when I depart from England, my aunt Betty will remain elusively here.

The Magic Mirror

The sparrow hops out on the bendy branch of the tree. My bib is grey and his is black. Patches of white on his cheeks. But I can't see my own face.

"Very ill," Sister Elspeth says to Sister Francis. She thinks I can't hear her bad breath whisper.

Blossoms the colour of tongues. "Is Mommy sick?"

"Be quiet, Betty. Attend to your work," Sister Elspeth says. These wet clothes. She wants to cut out my tongue. Her white hair could be a nest. Wound round and round the top of her bossy head. But Sister Francis smiles at me. "We'll go for a walk to the pier, after." A promise. I like the caramel spots on her hands.

But is Mommy sick? Do the laundry. Mommy too far away, with her canaries and violin. But the sparrow is here in the cherry tree. Black streaks on the brown feathers. Cheery blossoms, Daddy called them.

"Betty, don't just stand there. Who do you think you are? Queen Elizabeth the Second?"

Her hands are empty. But Sister Elspeth can't bend down, she says. The handle goes round and round with yellow strips. I lift the big basket of clothes up to my waist. With a helping hand from Sister Francis, up now on my shoulder. Fresh wet whiteness beside my face. Full. Not like Sister Elspeth's empty white hairy nest. This basket too heavy. I like the little one. But I am strong. Cheery blossoms.

Down the dark green hall that steals nearly all the light. I follow Sister Franny. She gets mad when I call her Sister Fanny. It moves from side to side like a horse. Clack, when she opens the door. Bright hot air falls out of the sky. My arms pulling from my body when we go over to the porch. A gull cries like it's hurt.

Drop the basket on the stool and hop up on the chair. I'm the queen of the castle. Her hand with the caramel bits that aren't sticky (but stick on). Gives me a wooden peg. Like a little man with two legs. But no noggin. An unmentionable, she calls these bloomers. I hang the dripping legholes on the line. Stick the stick man over top and push the line away. Bend over for more clothes. Not proper to talk about this one either. Is that the same gull crying? But here's a bright new wooden peg. Not dark and rain-rough. Socks, two by two. More two by two. The wet bedsheet needs lots of little men. One two three four and then I let the white wall blow away. Out to where I know the sea is coming in or going out. All done. "Sister?" She was staring down at the vegetable garden. Where soft new green things come out of the dry dirt.

The two of us walk back through the cool dark of the hall. Listening to our own footsteps on the hardness. Landing together.

The sparrow still here. Singing a song in the cheery cherry tree. More heavy clothes for the basket and Sister Elspeth. The sparrow has a secret nest. Under the eaves in back. Messy, with sticking-out bits. Not perfect like Sister Elspeth's hair. Eats bugs and seeds. I'd rather use the smaller basket. Once I saw one of its eggs. Not a soft soft blue shell like a robin's. Had speckles the colour of an olive. Remember the wet laundry, Sister Elspeth says, just with her face. Those eyes fixed on me. Wicker basket. Wicked girl.

The sparrow flies down. Holds his little wings out against the wind so he won't crash into the grass. A hurt leg? He hops over to taste the laundry paste. Leans his head down, looks sideways at me, then sticks his short bill into the glop. Pecks away at the paste. "Filthy little thing!" Sister Elspeth waves her arms up and down like a witch trying to fly. Grey feathers underneath when it soars, making him harder to see. She would cut his tongue out. Yes, the laundry. Devils devour her.

Daddy told me the story of the sparrow with the slit tongue. Before he went on a journey far far away to a cold mountain. You will be happier here, little daughter. Winter all the time up there. The sparrow has two baskets to give. One small, like a sparrow. That's the one to choose. Silver and gold, silks and candy inside. The big basket is for greedy ones. Full of scorpions and snakes and devils with burnt faces and black tails and pitchforks to jab you with. I don't like them. The sparrow is back in the cheery tree. He sings all the time.

"After this load, it will be time to get ready for our walk, Betty, by the strand."

Sister Franny helps me lift the smaller wicker basket. Water drips down my face. Falls from my eyes like I am crying. But the sparrow is singing and after we hang up these clean clothes, we will set out for the sea. And maybe get a Hastings rock?

First, though, I will take out the circle of shining metal with its handle. That shows me my face. Mommy told me if I wish to see her, just take out this mirror. Tell me your heart and I will hear you. It will never lose its roundness. The moon keeps missing part of itself. Sometimes it is cut like a melon. Sometimes it is sliced like a small lemon. But not the mirror. Hang this last one up to dry in the sunshine. And now I will go to my little room and take the mirror out of the box and ease her pain. I will see Mother's face again. Not old, not sick, but smiling and smooth and shining and beautiful.

Monday, June 16

In an act of male bonding and farewell, I walk with Antonio as he heads off to work via the East Finchley Station—a reversal of his greeting upon our arrival. An embrace before he heads south on the Northern Line, then I go back and check for email. The pleasure of a Father's Day greeting from Justin. My own father, who always made time to visit people in hospitals, has been dead of cancer of the esophagus nearly twenty years now, and I wish I could give him a hug on Father's Day.

Only one of my father's personal letters from Australia survives, its date unknown. How very short seems the distance between that little boy writing from Melbourne and the patient dying in Vancouver:

> "My dear Daddy
>
> "Thank you very much for the books and letter. We all had influenza one after another. Betty stayed at Aunty Mary's for a week while Mother was sick. We went to the Raymonds on Thursday. I learnt to ride a bike. Allan took us that is Noel and I, Mother and Betty did not come, to their new house. He showed me where the organ was going to be put. They have an orchard at the back

of their house. The apricots were ripe and we ate a lot. We had ice cream for supper. After supper we had a cricket match with Joyce, Allan and another girl. They made 8 in their 1st innings. We made 13. I made 10 and Noel made 3. They made 18 in their second innings. We made 33. Noel made 24 and I made 8 not out. I will write my report out on the next page. I hope you are quite well.

"Love from John"

Dad's good manners were evident until the very end, as he would excuse himself repeatedly in the cancer ward before spitting out into the basin. He'd agreed to make a demonstration video so other dying patients would be less scared.

Ann prints out a segment of the Paris map, showing the location of the Hotel Cosmos, our destination tonight—and every night? My pack is stuffed with Italian and British books and papers, the heaviest it's ever been. Our good-bye hugs to the-always-generous Ann, then Jo and I ride down to Waterloo Station. While she gets in line to pick up the chunnel tickets, I stand beside the two large packs.

Freed from habits of house and work in which days and months can register as little or nothing, travel gives back a felt duration: you get to live longer. Each half-startled moment of this journey has counted like a kid's—perhaps like Betty's? When you encounter the unknown, nothing is on cruise-control. The joy and achievement of travel is to cheat time, but I'm ready to return. These extra minutes of immobilized waiting, while Jo is in intense conversation with the agent, are tipping me over into boredom. Semi-drudgery looms as she begins talking to a second agent. I just want to be out of here now.

Yet I can't forget our over-the-top good fortune at sharing Ann and Antonio's lives for a week. And I can't begin to count the people who've given savour to this journey.

> As I was going to St Ives
> I met a man with seven wives.
> Every wife had seven sacks,
> Every sack had seven cats,
> Every cat had seven kits.
> Kits, cats, sacks and wives,
> How many were going to St Ives?

The answer to the riddle is—if you don't get distracted by mathematical calculations—one. Aside from the speaker, everyone was "met," going in the opposite direction, away from St Ives. Like so many riddles and nursery rhymes, it is disquieting: an unexpected aloneness revealed in the midst of what felt uncountable.

Betty, living in a child's mind, had all our relatives reaching out to her, from many continents—Asia, Australia, Europe, North America, Africa—fetching her across oceans. In that sense, she lived at the hub of the wheeling globe. My aunt's neighbourhood was the whole earth. And her mind illuminates the gappiness in everyone's travel, as we move both ignorantly and innocently, experiencing what we don't know. Maybe I created too large a myth out of my aunt, whose photo shows an ordinary woman, small and smiling.

If circumnavigating the earth has to be, implicitly, a quest for self-knowledge, I have found more incompleteness than I would have reckoned. And my sense of identity is messier than when I set out. Too many lives are rolled up inside me, I guess. A real mixture, like this world.

Jo—this amazing creature who I've known since grade four—is now talking patiently to a woman who looks like a supervisor, while I dream of Hornby Island. Of getting back to the Pacific Northwest Coast of my earliest childhood memories, where fir and arbutus embrace. A spirited reminder that I do not live alone but conjoined in a sharing of habitat: touching and coupling and growing separately together.

Finally, Jo steps away from the counter—and grins over at me. They cancelled our rail tickets for no reason, but my clever woman politely declined to sit on a jump-seat in the corridor or to take a later train. The result: we will ride to France first-class! Yes, I know I'm fortunate to have her to travel with through the years.

In this train car, a glass of champagne, white wine with mackerel hors d'oeuvres, Swedish pork balls, and chocolates, and all free. After the months of budget constraint we had before getting to England, this largesse is hilarious. But in the middle of what feels like a party, a young guy with a buzz-cut travelling to the Paris Air Show tells me that French air traffic controllers are going on strike, on June 19—our departure date for the flight home to Canada. We're still trying to circle this blue planet on its elliptical orbit.

I'm more than ready to retrace the steps to the large lantern of wood and glass resting on its side that is our luck to call home. And as the earth rolls towards darkness there, the immense, cliff-dwelling arbutus tree that was here six hundred years ago will catch reds and mauves in its arms.

Acknowledgements:

In an endeavour like this, it might be easier to list those who shouldn't be thanked. The individuals mentioned later in the book, I can only hope, will feel my gratitude adequately conveyed there. For those who don't appear in the narrated portions of the journey, my thanks here to Elke Rosendahl and Masoud Zadeh for their hospitality on Waiheke Island, N.Z., Brenda Cha and Peter Wardle for their warm welcome at Napier, N.Z., Karl Meier for sharing his place in Mackay, Queensland, and Fran Gerlan and Peter Sadler for scooping us away to their home at Crunella Beach, Australia.

As for the second, more fraught voyage, that of the writing, I'd like to thank Bob Burn-Murdoch, Curator of the Norris Museum, St Ives, and Jane Winter, Archives Assistant at the Huntingdon County Record Office. Thanks as well to Joan Gage for transcribing an inaudible tape and to Faye Landels for typing out an illegible notebook. My appreciation to my brother, Doug, my sister, Joan, to my cousins, Anne Wyness and Jane Babuin, and, foremost, my uncle Noel whose unstinting delight and vivid sharing kept this work alive. Very special gratitude to my father's "Cousin Rob" who a year after this narrated journey invited me to St Leonards-on-Sea, where he graciously and candidly spoke about our, at times, troubled family history.

Due in part to the rhetorical skills of Dean John Lepage, the space needed for this research was generously made available by Vancouver Island University through a travel grant and the funding of a term leave. Much appreciation to Kevin Roberts, whose many friendships in his native Australia meant I felt more like a guest than a tourist on that vibrant continent. Much gratitude once again to Gary Geddes, the publisher long ago of my first book, for reading more than one draft of this one, and for his nearly debilitating insights into how to make it better. Liza Potvin and Kate Braid, too, offered illuminating critical insights. To Hiro Boga, my former student, many thanks for teaching me so much about how this book might usefully be re-written. Final thank you to Ron Smith, longtime publisher and friend, for telling me where to go—for a possible structure: to John Berger's *From A to X : A Story in Letters*.

I would also like to thank Henning Nielsen for the cover design concept.

Parts of this tale of circumnavigation have appeared in a slightly different way in *Writing the West Coast* (2008), eds. Christine Lowther & Anita Sinner, at *Dis/solutions: The Future of the Past in Australia, New Zealand and the Pacific*. 10th EASA Conference, Mallorca, 2009, and in my fiction, *Elliot & Me* (2006), *Furry Creek* (1999), and *Crossing the Gulf* (1998).
Born in Vancouver,

Keith Harrison studied at UBC, Berkeley, and McGill writing a dissertation on Malcolm Lowry. Harrison has also written a group of stories, Crossing the Gulf (1998), which contains a piece that won the Okanagan Short Story Award, and he has edited an anthology of short fiction, Islands West: Stories from the Coast (2001). His five novels are Dead Ends (1981), a tale of two cities, Vancouver and Montréal; After Six Days (1985), about two contemporary couples; Eyemouth (1990), set mainly in Scotland during the French Revolution and its after-math and taking the form of letters; Furry Creek (1999), a documentary fiction exploring the life, death, and art of Pat Lowther; and Elliot & Me (2006), a doubled-voiced narrative about a mother and her teenaged son set on Hornby Island. Harrison's novels have been nominated for Books in Canada Best First Novel Award, QSPELL's Hugh MacLennan Fiction Prize, and the Ethel Wilson Award. Keith Harrison teaches at Vancouver Island University, and lives on Hornby Island, British Columbia.